Learning IBM Watson Analytics

Make the most advanced predictive analytical
processes easy using Watson Analytics with
this easy-to-follow practical guide

James D Miller

BIRMINGHAM - MUMBAI

Learning IBM Watson Analytics

First published: March 2016

Production reference: 1210316

Published by Packt Publishing Ltd.
Livery Place
35 Livery Street
Birmingham B3 2PB, UK.

ISBN 978-1-78588-077-3

www.packtpub.com

Credits

Author
James D Miller

Reviewer
Joy Mustafi

Commissioning Editor
Veena Pagare

Acquisition Editor
Manish Nainani

Content Development Editor
Viranchi Shetty

Technical Editor
Deepti Tuscano

Copy Editor
Vikrant Phadke

Project Coordinator
Izzat Contractor

Proofreader
Safis Editing

Indexer
Mariammal Chettiyar

Graphics
Disha Haria

Production Coordinator
Nilesh Mohite

Cover Work
Nilesh Mohite

About the Author

James D Miller is an IBM-certified expert, creative innovator, accomplished director, senior project leader, and application/system architect. He has over 35 years of extensive experience in application and system design and development across multiple platforms and technologies. His experience includes introducing customers to new technologies and platforms, integrating with IBM Watson Analytics, Cognos BI, and TM1. He has worked in web architecture design, systems analysis, GUI design and testing, database modeling, systems analysis, design and development of OLAP, web and mainframe applications and systems utilization, IBM Watson Analytics, IBM Cognos BI and TM1 (TM1 rules, TI, TM1Web, and Planning Manager), Cognos Framework Manager, dynaSight - ArcPlan, ASP, DHTML, XML, IIS, MS Visual Basic and VBA, Visual Studio, PERL, SPLUNK, WebSuite, MS SQL Server, ORACLE, SYBASE Server, and so on. James's responsibilities have also included all aspects of Windows and SQL solution development and design, such as analysis; GUI (and website) design; data modeling; table, screen/form, and script development; SQL (and remote stored procedures and triggers) development/ testing; test preparation; and management and training of programming staff.

His other experience includes the development of ETL infrastructure, such as data transfer automation between mainframe (DB2, Lawson, Great Plains, and so on) system and client/server SQL Server, web-based applications, and the integration of enterprise applications and data sources. James has been a web application development manager responsible for the design, development, QA, and delivery of multiple websites, including online trading applications and warehouse process control and scheduling systems, as well as administrative and control applications. He was also responsible for the design, development, and administration of a web-based financial reporting system for a 450-million dollar organization, reporting directly to the CFO and his executive team.

Furthermore, he has been responsible for managing and directing multiple resources in various management roles, including as project and team leader, lead developer, and application development director. James has authored *Cognos TM1 Developers Certification Guide*, *Mastering Splunk*, and a number of white papers on best practices, including *Establishing a Center of Excellence*. He continues to post blogs on a number of relevant topics based on personal experiences and industry best practices. James is a perpetual learner, continuing to pursue new experiences and certifications. He currently holds the following technical certifications: IBM Certified Business Analyst - Cognos TM1 IBM Cognos TM1 Master 385 Certification (perfect score of 100%), IBM Certified Advanced Solution Expert - Cognos TM1, IBM Cognos TM1 10.1 Administrator Certification C2020-703 (perfect score of 100%), IBM OpenPages Developer Fundamentals C2020-001-ENU (98% in exam), IBM Cognos 10 BI Administrator C2020-622 (98% in exam), and IBM Cognos 10 BI Professional C2020-180.

He specializes in the evaluation and introduction of innovative and disruptive technologies, cloud migration, IBM Watson Analytics, Cognos BI and TM1 application design and development, OLAP, Visual Basic, SQL Server, forecasting and planning, international application development, business intelligence, project development and delivery, and process improvement.

To Nanette L. Miller: "you are the answer to every prayer I've offered. You are a song, a dream, a whisper, and I don't know how I could have lived without you…"

About the Reviewer

Joy Mustafi has 15 years of experience in the industrial, research, and academic sectors.

He completed his graduation in statistics (2000) from Ramakrishna Mission Residential College, Narendrapur, West Bengal, and has a postgraduate qualification in computer applications (2003) from the Regional Computer Center, Kolkata. He won the Junior Research Fellowship award in computer and communication sciences from the Indian Statistical Institute (2004).

He joined IBM India in 2006 as an analytics consultant in the business analytics and optimization department. He has been associated with IBM - India Software Lab, Watson Business Group (2013) in continuing research and development of data mining, machine learning, and natural language processing. Joy moved to Global Technology Services in 2014, where he worked in the IT operations analytics department as a data scientist. He has also contributed as an SME to IBM Watson Analytics, IBM SPSS Statistics, IBM SPSS Modeler (with Text Analytics), and others.

He has been a visiting faculty member of different academic organizations. He has to his credit several patents and research publications on cognitive informatics and data science.

Joy founded MUST Research Club in 2015 to work in the field of computer science and informatics, mathematical science and statistics, cognitive science, and psychology. He is president of MUST Research Club, and he mentors technical students and early-level professionals to build their career in data science.

He was recognized as one of the top 10 data scientists in India in 2015 by *Analytics India Magazine* (http://analyticsindiamag.com/top-10-data-scientists-in-india-2015/).

MUST Research Club is dedicated to promoting excellence and competence in the field of cognitive computing and data science for the benefit of mankind. It aims to promote research and development in cognitive informatics in India and across the globe. It enables interaction between academic institutes and industries, helping them solve problems, as well as making them aware of the latest developments in the cognitive computing and data science sector. The purpose of this is to provide solutions, guidance, and training. MUST organizes lectures, seminars, and workshops, and collaborates on scientific programs and social missions. The most exciting feature of MUST is their fundamental research on cutting-edge technologies, such as data mining, machine learning, natural language processing, computer vision, speech technology, and other areas. The research team studies, invents, and improves technology tools and engineering techniques, and applies its intellect to the worldwide projects of MUST.

Joy also has a publication to his credit:

J. Mustafi; Natural Language Processing and Machine Learning for Big Data. Chapter of Techniques and Environments for Big Data Analysis, Springer International Publishing - Switzerland, 2016. [In Press]

My wife, Tanusree Mustafi, who is a psychologist by profession, helped me a lot in producing this book. In general, she always encourages me to study and invent more in the field of cognitive computing, data science, and advanced analytics, apart from my regular job. Both of us contribute significantly to MUST Research Club, along with other members of MUST.

www.PacktPub.com

eBooks, discount offers, and more

Did you know that Packt offers eBook versions of every book published, with PDF and ePub files available? You can upgrade to the eBook version at www.PacktPub.com and as a print book customer, you are entitled to a discount on the eBook copy. Get in touch with us at customercare@packtpub.com for more details.

At www.PacktPub.com, you can also read a collection of free technical articles, sign up for a range of free newsletters and receive exclusive discounts and offers on Packt books and eBooks.

https://www2.packtpub.com/books/subscription/packtlib

Do you need instant solutions to your IT questions? PacktLib is Packt's online digital book library. Here, you can search, access, and read Packt's entire library of books.

Why subscribe?

- Fully searchable across every book published by Packt
- Copy and paste, print, and bookmark content
- On demand and accessible via a web browser

Instant updates on new Packt books

Get notified! Find out when new books are published by following @PacktEnterprise on Twitter or the *Packt Enterprise* Facebook page.

Table of Contents

Preface

Based on deep technology experience and media publications, IBM Watson Analytics may be well positioned to *replace the data scientist* by providing the ability to perform sophisticated data discovery and analysis without all the complexity that usually goes along with it. Additionally, IBM is investing more and more each day into *cognitive computing*—Watson. Now they are even partnering leading technology universities to launch cognitive computing courses aimed at making this technology mainstream. This is the time to learn IBM Watson to compete in the world.

What this book covers

Chapter 1, A Quick Start, provides step-by-step instructions for accessing IBM Watson Analytics for the very first time. This chapter explains the different versions of IBM Watson that are currently available and important concepts and terminologies. It also makes recommendations for performing typical configurations or adjustments for use.

Chapter 2, Identifying Use Cases, uses realistic examples to explain how identifying use cases will help you better leverage IBM Watson Analytics to gain powerful insights from your data.

Chapter 3, Designing Solutions with Watson Analytics, covers the process of taking a sound approach to leveraging IBM Watson for content analytics, what to think about before you start, how to develop an *end-to-end solution design*, and how to set expectations for the resulting analysis.

Chapter 4, Understanding Content Analysis, discusses the practice of content analysis and how IBM Watson Analytics can be used as a tool to help analyze big data.

Chapter 5, Watson Analytics Predict and Assemble, leverages use cases to explore IBM Watson Analytics Predict and Assemble.

Chapter 6, Customizing and Extending, explores the concept of extending the power of Watson Analytics through the use of external tools such as IBM SPSS.

Chapter 7, Taking It to the Enterprise, prepares you to think from an *enterprise* perspective when using IBM Watson Analytics.

Chapter 8, Adding Value with Integration, discusses the importance of *integrating* Watson with various data sources, including IBM Cognos Business Intelligence (BI) reporting, and provides the steps required to perform such integrations.

What you need for this book

You will need a computer with an Internet connection!

Who this book is for

This book is for savvy business users as well as technical developers, or frankly anyone who wants to begin exploring the world of cognitive computing and add *valuable, cutting-edge expertise* to their resume.

Conventions

In this book, you will find a number of text styles that distinguish between different kinds of information. Here are some examples of these styles and an explanation of their meaning.

Code words in text, database table names, folder names, filenames, file extensions, pathnames, dummy URLs, user input, and Twitter handles are shown as follows: "The file, named `Historic_Stadium_Sales`, can be uploaded to Watson Analytics as explained in earlier chapters."

New terms and **important words** are shown in bold. Words that you see on the screen, for example, in menus or dialog boxes, appear in the text like this: "Create a free account by entering a valid e-mail address in the **Email address** space and clicking on the **Create Free Account** button, as shown in the following screenshot."

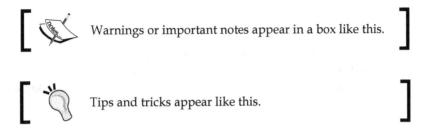

[Warnings or important notes appear in a box like this.]

[Tips and tricks appear like this.]

Reader feedback

Feedback from our readers is always welcome. Let us know what you think about this book—what you liked or disliked. Reader feedback is important for us as it helps us develop titles that you will really get the most out of.

To send us general feedback, simply e-mail feedback@packtpub.com, and mention the book's title in the subject of your message.

If there is a topic that you have expertise in and you are interested in either writing or contributing to a book, see our author guide at www.packtpub.com/authors.

Customer support

Now that you are the proud owner of a Packt book, we have a number of things to help you to get the most from your purchase.

Errata

Although we have taken every care to ensure the accuracy of our content, mistakes do happen. If you find a mistake in one of our books—maybe a mistake in the text or the code—we would be grateful if you could report this to us. By doing so, you can save other readers from frustration and help us improve subsequent versions of this book. If you find any errata, please report them by visiting http://www.packtpub.com/submit-errata, selecting your book, clicking on the **Errata Submission Form** link, and entering the details of your errata. Once your errata are verified, your submission will be accepted and the errata will be uploaded to our website or added to any list of existing errata under the Errata section of that title.

To view the previously submitted errata, go to https://www.packtpub.com/books/content/support and enter the name of the book in the search field. The required information will appear under the **Errata** section.

Piracy

Piracy of copyrighted material on the Internet is an ongoing problem across all media. At Packt, we take the protection of our copyright and licenses very seriously. If you come across any illegal copies of our works in any form on the Internet, please provide us with the location address or website name immediately so that we can pursue a remedy.

Please contact us at copyright@packtpub.com with a link to the suspected pirated material.

We appreciate your help in protecting our authors and our ability to bring you valuable content.

Questions

If you have a problem with any aspect of this book, you can contact us at questions@packtpub.com, and we will do our best to address the problem.

1
A Quick Start

This chapter will provide you with step-by-step instructions to access IBM Watson for the very first time, explain the different versions (of IBM Watson) that are currently available, and make recommendations for performing typical configurations or adjustments for use. We will *define the "Watson Analytic" landscape* by describing the current content analytics architecture, as well as introduce you to the most important concepts and terminologies needed to take advantage of Watson. Finally, we will wrap up with some helpful advice to go forward.

We'll break down the chapter like this:

- Step by step
- The content analytics architecture
- Important concepts and terminologies
- Generally good advice

Step by step

IBM Watson was named after IBM's first CEO and industrialist Thomas J. Watson. This supercomputing system was specifically developed to answer questions on a quiz show called *Jeopardy* in 2011, while celebrating the centenary year of IBM. During the last 5 years, IBM has been investing significantly in cognitive computing in business and technology and popularizing the brand name *Watson*, having multiple products with cognitive power. IBM Watson Analytics is one of the products by IBM, hosted on the cloud with useful analytics capabilities. In this book, most of the important features of Watson Analytics are described with illustrative examples and exercises.

If you haven't been exposed to IBM Watson before, the quickest and easiest way to get going is with the free cloud version. Google it, or (at the time of writing this book) you can visit http://www.ibm.com/analytics/watson-analytics/.

The site content found at this URL is updated regularly. At the time of writing this book, the following is the Watson Analytics page:

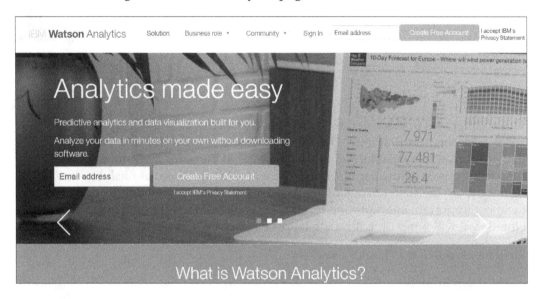

It's worth pointing out before we move on from this point that this website is full of valuable information — documents and videos — designed to give you all of the marketing and sales information that you want. I recommend that you take sometime and absorb what you can.

Signing up

The following are the steps to perform to access IBM Watson Analytics. It's quick and easy, so let's get started!

1. I always recommend that you read the privacy statement. This is accessed via a link in the top-right corner of the page: **I accept IBM's Privacy Statement**. This is important because while you are using Watson, IBM will be collecting your personal use information:

   ° To fulfill your requests

   ° To contact you for customer satisfaction surveys

   ° To support the products or services that you have obtained from IBM

- ° For marketing purposes
- ° To personalize your experience

2. Create a free account by entering a valid e-mail address in the **Email address** space and clicking on the **Create Free Account** button, as shown in the following screenshot:

3. From there, you will see the **Watson Analytics Registration Form**, which you will need to fill out—providing your e-mail address—as shown in this screenshot:

4. Once you click on the **Register** button, you will see the **Thank you for registering to use Watson Analytics** page, like this:

It's that easy! You are now an officially registered Watson user. You can now log in and start using the tool.

Logging in

Within a short period of time (after completing the registration process), you will receive the **Welcome to Watson Analytics** e-mail (sent to the e-mail account that you used during registration):

This e-mail will contain some helpful links, such as:

- The login (main page) URL (`https://watson.analytics.ibmcloud.com`)
- The Watson Analytics **Experts Blog**
- The Watson Analytics **Resources** and **Quick Find**

Use this e-mail to click on **just log in** and then bookmark the page in your favorite browser.

The welcome page

Let's explore the main page, or the welcome page, of IBM Watson Analytics.

Across the top of the page is the **Welcome** bar (or panel), as follows:

Things to know

- Clicking on **Welcome** (in the middle of the bar) always returns you to the welcome page.
- The name with which you registered will appear as the next link on the bar. Clicking on your name allows you to:
  - **My account**: Access information about your account
  - **Administer**: Administer your account
  - **Upgrade**: Upgrade your account (from the free versions of Watson)
  - **Logout**: Logout (of Watson)
- Clicking on the **?** sign will display the `docs/tours/hints` popup.
- Clicking on the far-right graph icon accesses the Watson **Collection** popup (collections will be discussed later in this chapter).

Your account

Clicking on your name and then on **My Account** will display the **User account** popup, as shown in the following screenshot. This popup will give you the total space allowed (based on your version of Watson) and the space you have used up to date:

Upgrading

If you are interested in upgrading (and you most likely will at some point), you can click on **Upgrade**. Watson then directs you to a contact page, where you can read (or talk to a person live) how and why to upgrade from your free vision of IBM Watson.

At the time of writing this book, IBM offers three versions:

- **Free Watson** (you're using it now; it is referred to as the **Freemium** version)
- **Personal**
- **Professional**

Basically, the difference between these versions is in the number of users allowed, the available space to store your data files and Watson's ability to *connect to* various data sources. Our freeware version basically forces us to use text/delimitated or CSV files and (of course!) Microsoft Excel files.

Learning more

In earlier versions of Watson, the **Main** or **Welcome** page included a **Learn more about** panel (shown in the next screenshot). This panel included a video link (a large panel to the left) and four subpanels that gave you quick access to the main functionalities of Watson:

- **Explore**: This is where you can add your data
- **Predict**: Use this to ask Watson to point out insights within your data files
- **Assemble**: Use Watson to create presentations of identified insights
- **Refine**: *Tweak* your data files for further discoveries:

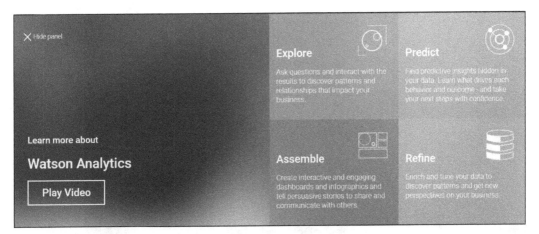

 This panel can be hidden and reshown whenever desired. In the updated version of Watson this panel has been removed, but you can find plenty of information to help you get started with using Watson under **Docs** and **Featured topics** (more resources exist, including a library of how-to videos, which we will cover in *Chapter 8, Adding Value with Integration*).

The shortcut panel bar

At the top of the welcome page, you will find Watson's shortcut panel bar, as shown in the following screenshot:

Using this panel, you can perform searches and access the **Add**, **Filter**, and **Sort** features of Watson:

- **Search**: Using the **Search** feature, you can quickly locate artifacts and information within the Watson environment. Simply start typing a text string to ask Watson to locate what you are interested in. Oddly, the panel search works differently from the **?** help mentioned earlier. For example, using the **?** help, you can add a wildcard as follows:
  - ° **CON***: The panel search does not support the wildcard, so the following works:

 Like most searches, clicking on the **X** sign to the right of the search box clears the typed text.

- **Add**: Clicking on **Add** (on the shortcut bar) displays the **Add** popup. Here, you use **Create something new** or **Or add your data**:

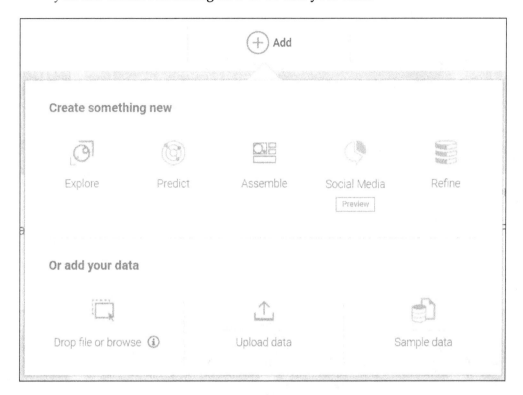

If you select **Add** and then **Create something new** without previously adding data (to the Watson environment), you won't be able to do much with **Explore**, **Predict**, **Assemble**, and **Refine**, so let's skip these (for the moment) and walk through the **Or add your data** section.

Starting by clicking on the left **Drop file or browse**, Watson presents a typical browse dialog so that you can locate a file to upload.

Let's walk through a quick, simple example. I have a file from a transportation-for-hire service with real-time information about the locations of its taxis, as shown in the following screenshot:

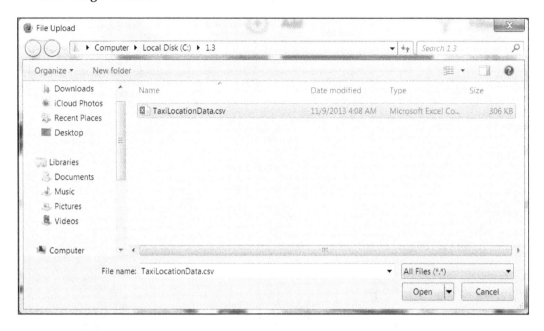

Once you select the file, Watson uploads it:

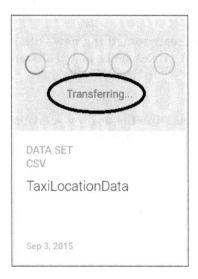

Once Watson is done uploading your data, it's ready for exploration (more about this soon)!

In addition to the **Drop file or browse** functionality, Watson provides an upload data (displayed in the bottom center of the **Add** popup). Clicking on this option displays a new and interesting popup:

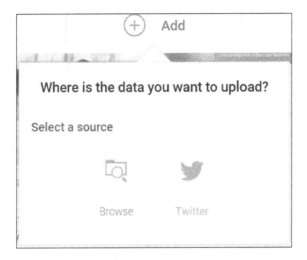

Browse provides the same functionality as described previously under **Drop file or Browse**, while **Twitter** is really an advertisement suggesting that you upgrade to a paid version of Watson; that is, if you click on **Twitter**, Watson will politely suggest that you upgrade your subscription level:

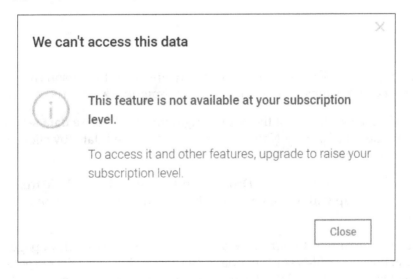

Explore, Predict, Assemble, and Refine

Now that we have (at least some) data in Watson, we can do something with it!
Let's start by clicking on **Explore**. This will open the **Create new exploration** popup
(shown here):

On this popup, you will see a list of files already uploaded to Watson (we only have
one so far—**TaxiLocationsData**—so it's a pretty straightforward process to find it).

A search is located at the top of the popup (right under **Choose a data set**), and
you can sort the list of files by **Name**, **Type** or the **Modified** date (by clicking on the
respective column title).

Can't see your file? You can access **Drop file or browse** or **Upload file** from the
bottom of this popup without having to go back to the **Main** or **Welcome** page and
adding it.

Once you click on **to select** your file, Watson displays the **Exploration** page, where
you can establish your file's starting points. Starting points are a list of (potentially)
interesting facts about your data. These facts can lead you to expose additional
particulars about your data that may not have been initially obvious.

Watson may provide one or more starting points (depending on your data), which you can select to **get going**, or you can establish your own (starting points) by **asking a question**. In our data example, Watson tells us, **There are no starting points that match your keywords**, like this:

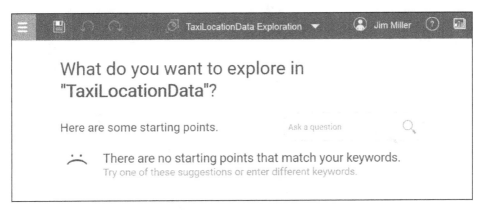

By using Microsoft Excel, I know a few things about the data—what fields (**Timestamp**, **Latitude**, **Longitude**, **Device_ID**, and **DATA_SOURCE**) are in the file and how many rows (5,487) there are in the file. But does Watson know? Let's see…

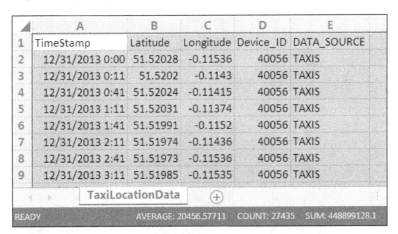

First, notice that across the bottom of the page is now a **field ticker**, which lists each field that Watson found in our file as well as any fields that it can derive, for example **Year**, **Month**, and **Day** (all derived from the **Timestamp** field):

Let's start by asking a simple question about one of the fields: **what fields are in timestamp**. To do this, I just type my question as if I were asking a human and click on the blue magnifying glass icon (on the right). Watson quickly responds with several suggestions for starting points, as follows:

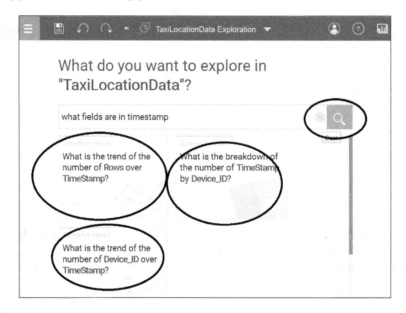

You can click on any of the starting points to begin your exploration. Starting with the upper-left option (**What is the trend of the number of Rows over Timestamp?**), Watson displays this:

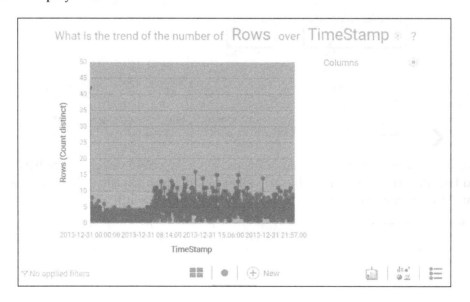

Let's dissect what Watson has provided; the following is the page separated into four sections:

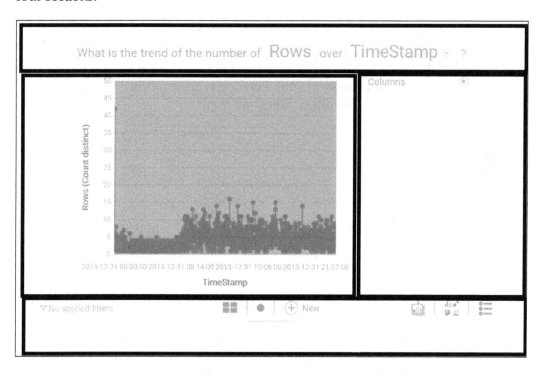

Across the top of the page is the original starting point question, in the left-middle is the visual representation of the result (of the starting point question), in the right-middle is the visualization configuration section, and across the bottom is the starting point tool bar:

- **Original starting point**: Notice that the field names from the file that are part of the original starting point question are hyperlinks. Clicking on these fields allows you to change the file field reference. Clicking on the circled **X** mark on the right of the section clears the starting point question.

- **Visual representation**: This is Watson's visualization for the starting point question based on our data.

- **Visualization configuration**: This is where you can modify the Watson visualization by clicking on the gear icon in the top-right corner. Watson allows you to filter the selected visualization columns and add or remove columns. The visualization value can also be changed.

  ○ **Starting point toolbar**: The starting point toolbar is made up of three action sections. They are **Filter** (far left), **Navigate** (middle) and **Administer** (far right): Filtering is accomplished by selecting a column and defining a filter condition:

  ○ **Navigate** allows you to switch between a thumbnail view and the current page view or (add) a **New** exploration view:

  ○ **Administer** provides the ability to add a selected exploration to a Watson collect (of explorations), change visualization types, and set specific options for the selected visualization type:

- **Filter**: Back on the Watson shortcut bar is **Filter**. This feature allows you to set what Watson displays for you on the welcome (or main) page. By default, Watson is set to show **All** (as indicated by the check mark to the left of the selection), which means that you'll see panels for your datasets, explorations, predictions, views, and even social media projects. Once you become more familiar with Watson, and based on what you may be currently working on, you may want to clear the page and show only the panels that you are interested in. Simply clicking on **Filter** and then on the panel type (or types) that you want Watson to display will refresh the welcome page to the desired view:

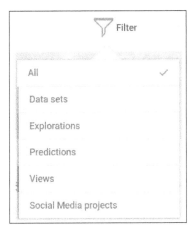

- **Sort**: Also available on the shortcut bar is **Sort**. It allows you to organize the panels on the welcome (or main) page by displaying them:

    ° In alphabetical order
    ° By the last modified date
    ° By the date of creation

Although there is still quite a lot more to learn, we've now touched on the basic mechanisms of the IBM Watson interface. So, we will move on to a discussion on the content analytics architecture. In later chapters of this book, using case studies, we will provide more details.

The content analytics architecture

Before getting started with any new tool, it's wise to spend some time and understand how the tool is constructed, or made up, and how it works. In this section, we'll go over the general architecture of IBM Watson and provide a short description of each architectural component along with the flow between those components.

The main components

Watson is built using a robust content analytics architecture made up of the following components:

- Crawlers
- Document processors
- Indexers
- A runtime search engine
- A content analytics miner
- An administration console

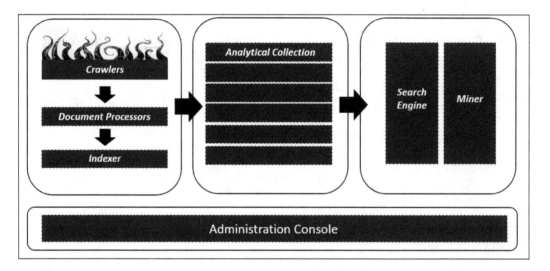

Crawlers

As the name implies, crawlers *crawl through* what is known as a *crawl space* (one or more defined sources for data) and *extracts content* from those sources. A Watson administrator can define rules that direct *crawling behavior*. Crawling behavior is defined as configuring how a crawler will effect (system) resources and which sources for data a crawler will use.

You can start and stop your crawlers by hand, or you can schedule a crawler by telling it when it must run for the first time and at what interval thereafter.

Document processors

The document processor component processes *crawled documents* and prepares them for indexing by applying various *text analytics* to the documents. Basically, what is happening is that each text analytic applied to a document *annotates the document* with additional information (inferred from the document), which helps explain what is in the document and perhaps makes it more valuable and *indexable*. This is the high-level explanation.

The process of applying these text analytics can be thought of as a *pipeline* where crawled documents enter. Then they are *parsed*. Finally, a prearranged number of (text analytics) *annotators* process and remove what is needed from the document.

Indexers

The indexer component takes the parsed (or annotated) documents and builds an *index on your content* to improve performance during text mining and analysis. Once you start an indexer, it will automatically index each document (after the document is processed by the document processors).

Note that changes made to crawled documents can be included in the index either by manually performing an *index rebuild* or by setting the options in the collected documents so that the changes are automatically retrieved and made a part of the index.

Search engine

The search engine is server-based. This is a component that facilities all user search and analytics requests. The content analytics miner (explained in the next section) is an example client application that makes requests to the search engine. Depending on various factors, such as the size and user base of an environment, more than one search engine may be used.

Miner (content analytics)

The miner uses a browser-based interface and is used to perform content analysis. Using the miner, client requests are made to the search engine, which carries out your requests on your analytical collections.

Administration console

The administration console (like the miner) is a browser-based component that is used to administer your collections, monitor system activities and logs, and set up users, the search engine, and the miner.

The flow of data

IBM Watson utilizes highly indexed document content called **collections** for text mining and content analysis. Administrators create, configure, and manage the content analytics collections so that analysts can utilize the miner to analyze data that is in the collections. The *flow* — through the components described earlier in this chapter — from the creation of a collection through the content's availability for analysis is described as follows:

1. A collection is created.

2. Crawlers are configured for the collection.

3. Crawlers routinely extract data from the defined data sources and store the data as documents (in a cache on the disk).

4. All documents are read by the document processors.

5. The document processors run text analytics against the content to prepare the content for indexing.

6. Documents are saved in the content collection.

Steps 3 to 6 will be a continuous operation until all the documents are read by the crawlers and then stored in the index of the specified collection.

Once you have built a content collection, it is immediately available for analysis.

Exiting the flow

Along the flow, there are three points where extracts can be created to export documents for importing into external systems:

*   After documents have been crawled and stored (in binary form)

*   After indexing (in binary form, with annotations added by the text analysis annotators)

*   After a search has been completed (from the miner, you can export the current search results set)

Deep inspection

This feature must be enabled for a collection by the administrator and is similar to exporting documents. You may use this feature if the number of keywords is so large that it may impact the system's performance while using the analytics miner. Deep inspections are not possible through the miner.

Important concepts and terminologies

Now that we've covered the architecture and flow, let's go over a number of concepts and terms that you should be aware of.

Structured versus unstructured

Unstructured (sometimes called textual) information is generally **natural** or **free** text. It is understood simply by people but is usually problematic for computer processing. In contrast, structured information is *easily processed* by a computer.

Text analytics

This is a term that refers to automated methods of converting unstructured data into structured data.

Searching

When you search, you already have something in mind that you are looking for, and your task is to create a search query that can locate an exact or partial match of your target.

Discovery

Discovery refers to an *exploratory exercise* that is goal driven—this is what Watson refers to as *starting points* used to learn more about a specific topic.

Mining

Data mining is a method of locating *patterns* or insights within data. Data mining is a natural part of discovery.

Collections

An analytics collection is a grouping of documents that are indexed and available for search and analysis.

Facets

Facets represent the different characteristics of a collection and are used to *navigate* and *analyze* the collection with the miner. *Default facets* are created automatically for each collection. In addition, facets can be loaded with information obtained directly from structured data fields in your collection or with actual information from the text. Facets allow you to focus on only those documents that you are interested in.

Frequency

Frequency represents the current number of documents that contribute to a selected keyword. This is useful in identifying trends in the collection.

Correlation

Correlation measures how well a *facet* (defined previously) is related to a query or criteria.

Deviation

Deviation is a weighted moving average that measures the average change in a facet. It measures how facets deviate from the *average frequency* over a specific time period.

Generally good advice

Now that we've got you started by accessing Watson for the first time, defined the architecture used, and explained the key concepts and terms, here is some good advice to be used as we continue our journey.

Hints

Some basically overlooked advice is always to *read the documentation!* Seriously, until you become more comfortable with Watson, **Show hints**. IBM Watson does a nice job of *pointing the way through the interface* if you let it. To *show the hints*, click on **Show hints**:

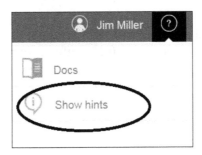

Join in

Also under the **?** icon, you can access **Community** (shown here):

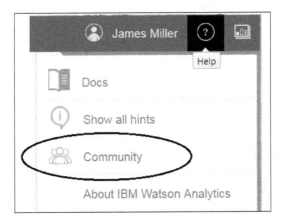

Before going much further, it is a very good idea to establish yourself within the IBM Watson community. You already have a user ID (used when you registered), so log in and explore. Among many other reasons, this is where you will be able to find plenty of product support. As said by them:

> *"When you need assistance to understand a particular feature, have encountered a technical issue, or have an issue with your log in or IBM ID, here are some places to find answers and get help..."* – IBM Watson Support.

Summary

In this chapter, we got you started with IBM Watson by guiding you through the registration and welcome process, and then pointed out the basic features of Watson's web interface. Next, we reviewed the architecture that Watson is based on as well as introduced some important concepts and terms associated with the product and technology.

In the next chapter, we will explain how identifying *use cases* will help you to better leverage the technology and gain powerful insights using IBM Watson.

2
Identifying Use Cases

In this chapter, we will explain how identifying use cases will help you *better leverage the technology* of IBM Watson Analytics to gain powerful insights through content analytics. This chapter will also cover how to *ask the right questions of data* and ensure that the *correct context* is used during analysis. Several real-life scenarios will be cited and explained.

This chapter is broken down like this:

- Defining a use case
- What to ask about your data
- Putting data in to context
- Working use case examples

Defining a use case

First, we'll assume that you have at least a general understanding of what a *use case* is and perhaps only require the generally accepted definition of the term as a reminder:

> *"A use case is a list of action or event steps, typically defining the interactions between a role (known in the Unified Modeling Language as an actor) and a system, to achieve a goal" – Systems Modeling Language (SysMl).*

Effectively, a use case is a *true-to-life* situation that occurs within your organization or field of interest. These common situations or scenarios (or collections of scenarios) are opportunities in which Content Analytics (IBM Watson Analytics) can be used to provide actionable results and insights.

Importance of use cases

Use case *scenarios* are normally user concentrated, provide easily understood narratives, promote quality, and facilitate validation:

- **User concentration**: A use case definition begins with the identification of an *actor* interacting with a process or system with an *intended goal in mind*.

- **Understandable narratives**: Use cases are generally *written* in a *natural*, textual form, yielding a *legible requirement* — not computer code — so it's understandable by everyone.

- **Promotion of quality**: The development of a use case can be accomplished using a *standard template* that consists of a *basic flow* and *exception flows*. This is a structured and beneficial way to get clear, stable, and high quality requirements systematically.

- **Facilitation of validation**: A use case facilitates straightforward derivation of functional test cases directly from the use cases providing a process for easy validation of assumptions or results.

By developing *use case scenarios*, you develop a deep understanding of your need or opportunity — *detailed requirements* for a new order processing system for an example, or maybe the *insight* you achieve from the process of creating a use case — based on your information (or data).

Working with Watson

The actor in your use case scenario has an objective. Through (most likely) a series of interactive steps, it consumes information. It interprets and evaluates that information to make a decision and, hopefully, provide awareness that is not previously known (that is, *an insight*). Watson Analytics *learns* in the same manner.

It observes, interprets, and evaluates the data to help *you* make better and more informed decisions and presumably provide better or more reliable *insights*. The magic is that this learning process is all performed at a scale never imagined before!

Your established use case scenarios can translate directly into the *where and how* IBM Watson Content Analytics can be of help to you. This information will be the basic design for your Content Analytics solution.

What to ask of your data

Insights derived through any learning process depend on the questions you ask of data and the context of that data (within your particular use case scenario). For example, let's say a use case involves the sales of team merchandise at the gates of a **National Football League** (**NFL**) stadium. Information (data) that shows weekly sales from the last few seasons' home games is provided. What insights can this data provide for the team?

Rather than starting by sorting, filtering, and pivoting data, perhaps using a programming language such as Perl or Python, wouldn't it be a better idea to use *the language and keywords of your business* to *ask data questions* that explore and visualize the data into answers?

IBM Watson Analytics does just this and even uses your data questions to generate a list of *starting points*, each of which opens a specific visualization.

The Watson Analytics interface gives three ways to get started with *questioning your data*. You can do any of these:

- From the welcome or main page, click on **Explore**, select a dataset, and enter a question

- From the welcome page, click on **Add**, then click on **Exploration**, select a dataset, and enter a question

- In **Explore**, click on **New** and enter a question

Building questions

To create a question in Watson Analytics to ask your data, you need to use *keywords*, *names of columns* (or fields) in your data, and *data values*:

- **Keywords**: These are used to format the visualization. Keywords are typically placed near the beginning of the question and are chosen from a list provided by Watson Analytics.

- **Names of columns**: These are also referred to as column titles. You can use one, two, or three column titles in a question. You can check your data file or use the Watson Analytics data tray to quickly view the available column titles and data values in your dataset.

- **Data values**: These are actual data values from your dataset for focusing on a specific piece of information, for example, to include a specific product name from a **Product** column, or a specific year value from a **Year** column. Data values are typically placed at the end of the question.

So for instance, in our stadium example, we can start by asking the question: what is the breakdown of sales by *gate number* for the *team hat*?

In the preceding question, notice that I have used the keyword *breakdown*, the fields in my file (column titles) are *sales* and *gate number*, and the data value I'm interested in corresponds to a particular product— *team hat*.

IBM Watson Analytics *processes* your question in the following way:

1. Watson Analytics matches the words in your question to the column titles in your dataset.

2. The remaining words in your question are matched to the actual data values in your dataset.

3. Keywords are used to select and format the visualization.

We'll provide more details on *building questions* in the *use case example* section of this chapter.

Putting data into context

A critical mistake is to treat all data the same and use the same *learning processes* to consume and visualize it. Even with similar data, *sales information*, for example, could vary widely based on **who** collected it, **what** the data is about, **when** it was collected, **why** it was collected, and **how** it was collected:

- **Who**: With the use of our stadium example, the sales information provided by *the stadium owner's organization* as opposed to *that solicited from independent sellers* may be quite different. In addition to who collected the data, who the data is about is also important. If the sales are reported on *higher dollar merchandise* verses *dollar items*, the count may be based on a sample rather than a *physical count*.

- **What**: Ultimately, you want to know what your data is about, but before you can do that, you should know what surrounds the numbers, or what the data represents in the world. In our example, does it make sense if our data is one week's worth of sales (as compared to) or one season's?

- **When**: Most data is linked to time in some way in that it might be a time series or a snapshot from a specific period. In both cases, you have to know when the data was collected. In our example, sales from 5 years ago when the team had a winning season may not be reflected in or compared to the current season when the team is losing games (and perhaps fans).

- **Why**: It's also important to know the reason the data was collected, mostly as a sanity check for bias. Sometimes, data is collected, or even fabricated, to serve an agenda, and you should be wary of these cases. Again, in our example, the sales reported by a particular product supplier (team hats) may be intended to influence the stadium owner to order more products from them.

- **How**: The *how* is often skipped since it tends to be complex and for a technical audience, but it's important to know how the data of interest was collected. Data scanned at registers as sales occur might be more enlightening then data manually collected from shelf stockers at the end of a day.

A final thought: learn all that you can about your data before anything else, and your analysis and visualization will be better.

Importance of data context

Without context, data can easily be misinterpreted and therefore be unusable. If the data is unusable, then any report or visualization based on it will also be unusable. As always, bad data is worse than no data.

Use case examples

This section presents examples of potential real-life scenarios in which Content Analytics might be used to provide actionable results and insights. Hopefully, as you read through these use cases, you'll gain a better understanding of how IBM Watson Analytics can be used.

Our first example is somewhat traditional in that we are exploring sales data and creating visualizations that will, hopefully, provide some insights.

NFL stadium sales

The owner or manager of a stadium where an NFL team plays its home games is trying to understand how its on-site merchandise sales are doing. The relevant data has been collected; it includes stadium sales by product for the last 13 home games. Let's use Watson Analytics to see what the data may tell us.

From the **Welcome** screen, click on **Add** and then click on **Drop file or browse**. From there, I browse to my file (`2015_StadiumSales.csv`) and select it. IBM Watson Analytics adds the file to our environment:

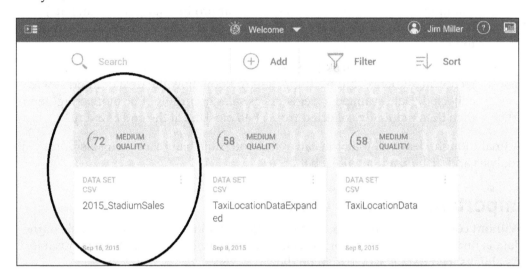

If we click on our file, we are ready to ask a question (or explore the *starting points* that Watson has already prepared for us).

Rather than start with our own question, we can scroll through Watson Analytics' starting points by clicking on the **>** icon. I've selected an interesting one — **What is the contribution of Quantity over Week by Stand Location?** (Check out the following screenshot):

After we have clicked on this starting point, Watson Analytics shows us a visualization answering that question, as follows:

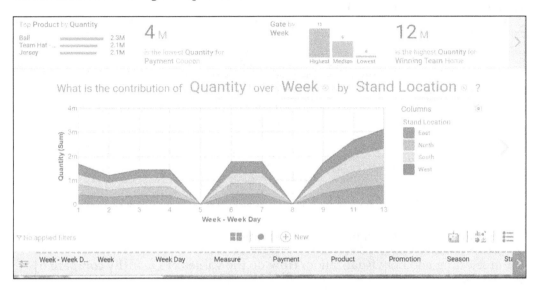

Watson Analytics has selected a recommended visualization (an area chart), but you can change it by clicking on the **Visualization type's** icon in the bottom-right corner, as shown in this screenshot:

Watson Analytics also gives us a number of insights about our data across the top of the page, like this:

You can scroll through to explore them, click to highlight, or, if you like, send to a new page. I'm interested in the weather's effect on the sales, so I click on **How do the values of Quantity compare by Weather**:

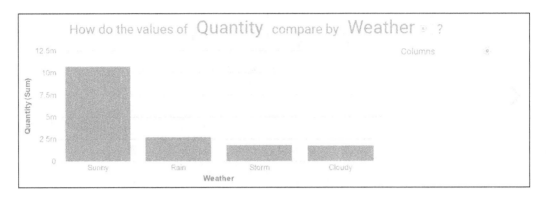

It seems like the fans buy more when it's sunny.

Upon selecting another visualization, **How do the values of Quantity compare by Week?**, we get this:

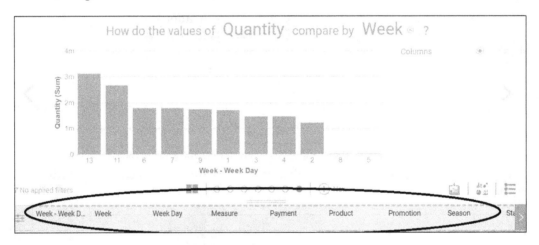

Notice that across the bottom, Watson Analytics displays our list of columns (fields) from our file. If we want to, we can select a column (let's try **Payment**) and drop it onto our visitation. Watson Analytics instantly resets our visualization to include **Payment**, as follows:

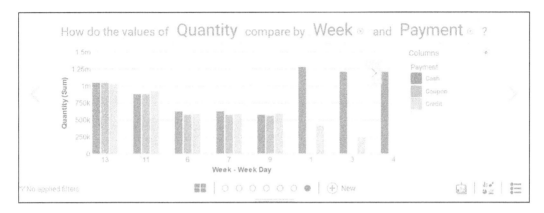

Let's try adding a filter. You can click on the filter icon (in the bottom-left corner of the page) and then click on **Add a filter**:

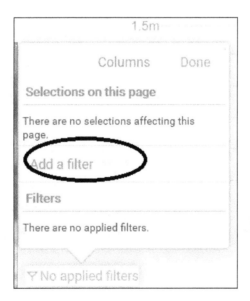

From there, select the **Weather** column and then check **Sunny**. Then click on **Done**, as shown here:

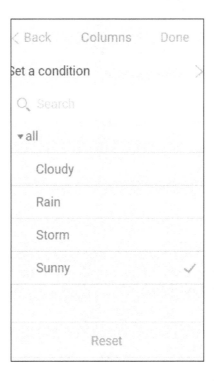

Again, Watson Analytics resets the visualization (with the filter applied), like this:

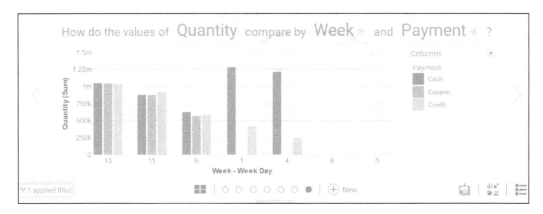

But enough of Watson Analytics' starting points. Let's create some questions of our own. Let's click on the > (next page) icon to the right of the current visualization:

IBM Watson Analytics will ask us, **What do you want to explore next?** (Check out the next screenshot):

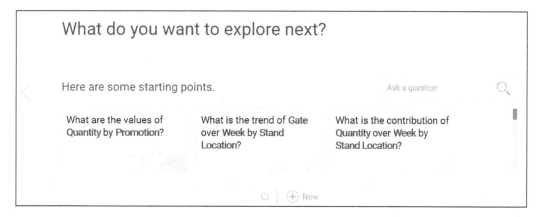

So let's ask some questions.

I am convinced that the weather is affecting my sales. I have seen that when it's sunny, fans purchase more merchandise. Let's go further with that idea. Does the weather affect the type of product purchased? I type my question, **what is the comparison of quantity by weather over product?** With that, Watson Analytics rephrases my question a bit and then provides a visualization:

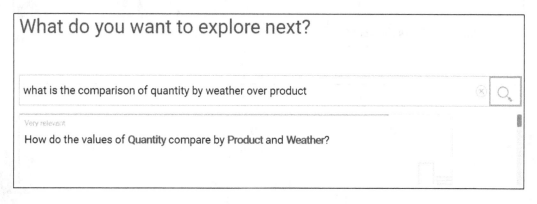

And when we click on the visualization, we get this:

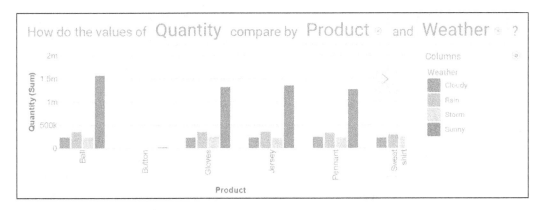

Let's try once more. You can click on the **+ New** icon to open a new page:

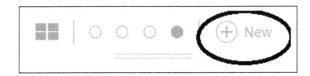

How about we try something trending? If I type **What is the average quantity by week by stand location**, Watson Analytics again rephrases my question and runs another visualization for me:

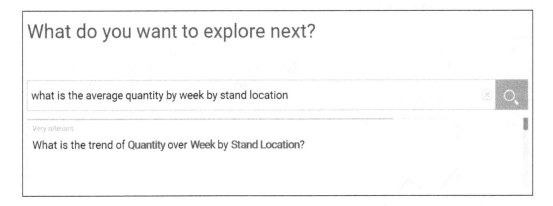

And now, let's look at the visualization!

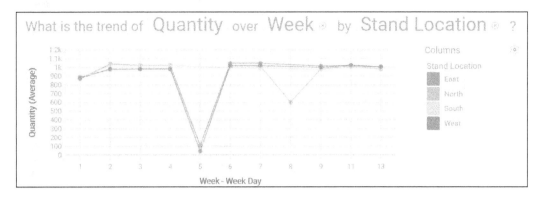

This gives us a pretty good idea about the average sales per week by our stand location. Next is the same visualization as an area chart, but filtered by stand location (to show only a single stand location, that is, north, and with **Payment type** included as an additional column):

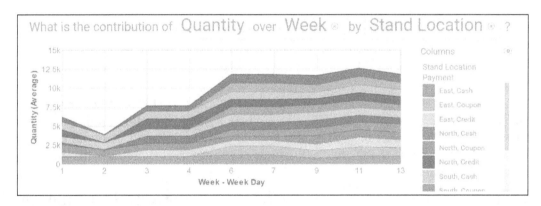

As you can see, there are still plenty of options to explore with this data, but for now, we'll move on to our next example use case.

Profitable slot machines

Another use case that we can consider to further explore Watson Analytics is of a gaming company that deploys a variety of slot machines in a multitude of ways. The company has a file containing the actual results by machine over a period of time, categorized by months and the days of the week. In the file are the particulars of each machine (type, theme, number of years the machine has been in service, and so on). Without diving into too much information about the file, let's do some exploration to see what insights Watson Analytics can give us about the gaming industry.

Using the same method as we did earlier (from the welcome page, click on **Add**, then on **Upload data**, we can add our slots' results (CSV) file to the Watson Analytics environment:

Quality

Before we move on, notice that this file is labeled **HIGH QUALITY**. What does this mean? It means that Watson Analytics does a better job of providing predictions and explorations if the quality of your data is high. The lower the quality of your data, the lower the accuracy of the analyses in your explorations and predictions (this is true for any tool).

In addition, Watson Analytics *scores* your data's quality (that is, the number to the left of **HIGH QUALITY**). The lower your data's score, the higher the number of outliers, missing values, and so on found in your data.

Always try to improve the quality of your data before you import it by:

- Removing blank rows from your data file
- Removing summary rows and columns from your data file
- Eliminating nested column headings and nested row headings

Refining data

To refine your data, click on the **Refine** icon (shown here):

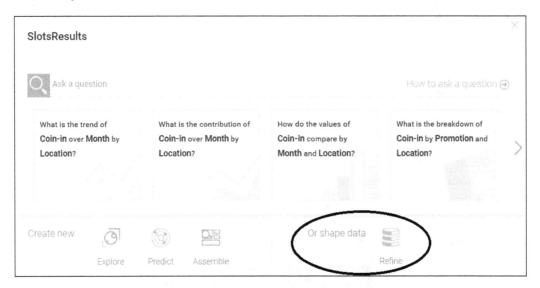

You can utilize Watson Analytics to improve the quality of your data. Once you upload your file, rather than *jumping into* the explorations, you can click on **Or shape data - Refine** (shown in the preceding screenshot):

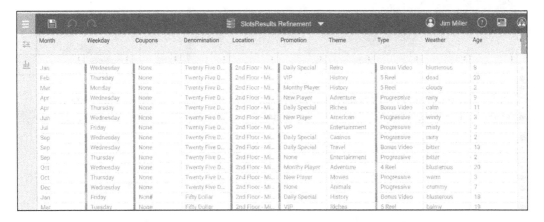

When you click on **Refine**, IBM Watson Analytics displays your data on the **Refinement** page (shown in the preceding screenshot). From there, you can review your data and, if needed, adjust it to your needs.

All of your adjustments are saved as *separate versions* of your original data.

There are different ways by which you can refine (and perhaps *better prepare*) your data. You can:

- Add calculations
- Filter data
- Rename columns
- Change data types
- Modify default aggregations
- Create hierarchies and groups

So let's experiment with some of these **Refine** or **Preparation** actions. To begin, in the top-left corner, you can click on the **Actions** icon, as shown here:

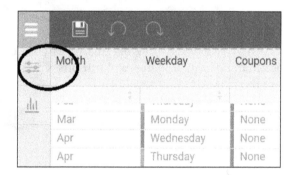

Clicking here opens the Watson Analytics *action center* (again, shown in the next screenshot), where you can see your **columns** and **rows** listed, along with various *other icons*:

Here is a list of various actions:

1. You can remove a row or column by unchecking that field (click on the *checkmark* to the left of the row or column name).

2. You can rename or filter a row or column by clicking on the *bar icon* to the right of the row or column and using the **Properties** dialog. This is illustrated here:

To change a field name, you must first click on **Change Name** and then type your new field name. To filter by the selected field, click on the **Select value** icon. Changing field names becomes particularly important if your field headings are non-descriptive, as they can be dependent on the source. Using non-descriptive field names lessens the impact of the visualizations created by Watson Analytics, since it's more difficult to relate to a query such as **how does the number of rows compare to 123** than something more readable, such as **how does the number of rows compare to Location.**

3. Create a new column calculation by clicking on **Calculation** (shown next):

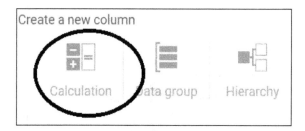

4. After you've clicked on **Calculation**, you can use the **Calculation** dialog (again, shown in the next screenshot) to create your expression:

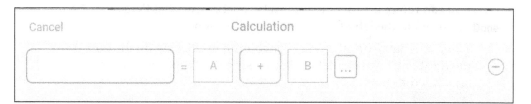

5. Create a data group by clicking on **Data group**:

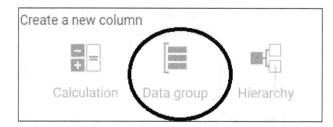

6. From the **Data group** dialog, you can select any number of fields to create a meaningful data group:

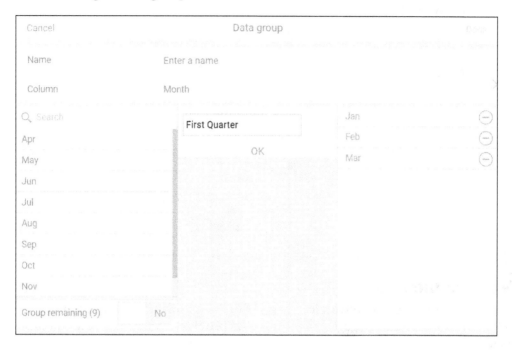

7. Create a hierarchy by clicking on **Hierarchy** (shown here):

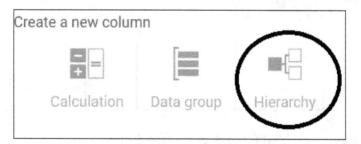

8. From the **Hierarchy** dialog (shown in the next screenshot), you can create an *organized view* of associated data from your file by adding and subtracting as many levels as you need:

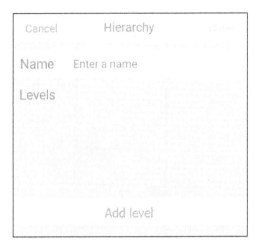

Viewing metrics

If you click on the **Data Metrics** icon (circled in the following screenshot) in the top-left corner of the refine page, Watson Analytics provides real-time metrics on the fields in your data:

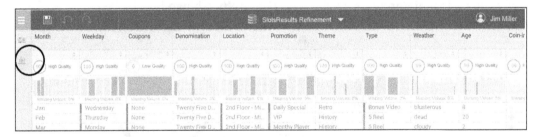

Metric information provided for each column includes:

*   A quality score (similar to the overall file quality score discussed earlier in this chapter)
*   The percentage of missing data
*   Distribution graphs of the data (only for numeric values)

Additional refinement actions include the following:

- Previews (by scrolling columns and rows)
- Sorting by columns by clicking at the top of a column
- The order of columns may be changed (by dragging and dropping)
- To save the file with a different name, you can click on the **Save** icon

More questions

Let's get back to exploring our slot machine. As already covered, IBM Watson Analytics reads your data and, based on its contents, provides a variety of questions (or *starting points*). In our slots example, Watson Analytics provides questions such as **What is the trend of Coin-in over Month by Location**.

In this example, the words **Coin-in**, **Month**, and **Location** are in bold. These indicate field names (columns) within our data. In addition, the word trend is used. Trend is an IBM Watson Analytics *visualization keyword*.

Keywords are used by Watson Analytics to format a visualization, and each has a different influence on how your data is retrieved and how the resulting visualization is created. IBM Watson Analytics provides the following keywords: compare, trend, contribution, correlation, relationship, breakdown, grouping, where, when, how long, average, total, maximum, minimum, top, bottom, best, worst, highest, lowest, most, least, rows, how many, and count.

Creating questions can be simple or challenging based on your needs. For example, if I were thinking in SQL terms, I might want to create a *group by query* to get the number of rows by location. In Watson Analytics, if I ask, **What is the number of rows by location**, Watson Analytics reformats my query as follows:

How does the number of rows compare by location?

Then it provides the following visualization:

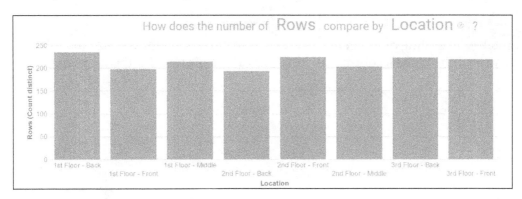

You can see the *somewhat* different mindset for formatting the query. Something else that's *fun* is Watson Analytics' ability to *think forward* as you start typing a question. For example, I typed **what is the average** and paused. Watson Analytics read my (partial) query and made this suggestion (as well as several others):

What is the trend of Coin-in over Month by Weather? The presentation given for this suggestion is as follows:

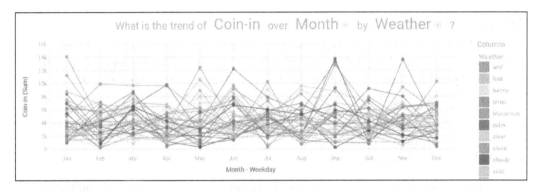

Remember that from the visualization, you can delete highlighted keywords or change them simply by clicking on them. The following is what I got when I clicked on the keyword **Weather** and selected **Type** from the field list:

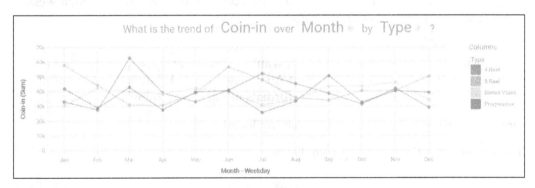

Another interesting question made using our slots data might be **what slot theme generated the highest coin-in value?** Here is a visualization for this question:

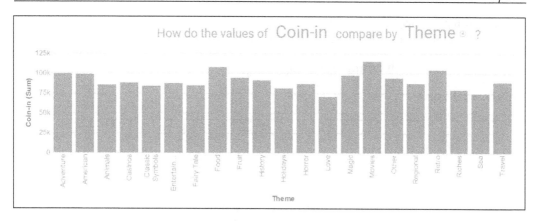

From the preceding data, it looks as if slot machines that offer a movie or food theme may be the most profitable. You can see that plenty of questions or *starting points* can be visualized based on the use of Watson Analytics' keywords. It's recommended that you take your time and experiment with each of the keywords to get a feel of how they can be used and what to expect as far as the results are concerned.

Let's move on to one more use case example before we wrap up this chapter.

Crime recording

Another *use case* might involve a file of criminal offenses or *crimes* reported over a period of time within a particular city's limits. The file lists a description (of the crime) the date the crime took place, a city district, beat, city grid, a universal **NIC** code, as well as GPS information (**latitude** and **longitude**).

Here is a section of the file:

cdatetime	address	district	beat	grid	crimedescr	ucr_ncic_c	latitude	longitude
1/1/2006 0:00	3108 OCCIDENTAL DR	3	3C	1115	10851(A)VC TAKE VEH W/O OWNER	2404	38.55042	-121.391
1/1/2006 0:00	2082 EXPEDITION WAY	5	5A	1512	459 PC BURGLARY RESIDENCE	2204	38.4735	-121.49
1/1/2006 0:00	4 PALEN CT	2	2A	212	10851(A)VC TAKE VEH W/O OWNER	2404	38.65785	-121.462
1/1/2006 0:00	22 BECKFORD CT	6	6C	1443	476 PC PASS FICTICIOUS CHECK	2501	38.50677	-121.427

It might be interesting to use Watson Analytics to do some exploration of this information!

After we've added it to the Watson Analytics environment (in the previously described method of browse and upload), let's see how we can visualize what type of *crime wave* we may have on our hands.

First, I want to know the total *number of crimes reported* (the number of rows or records in the file would indicate this), so I ask Watson Analytics:

What is the value of the number of Rows?

This is what I get:

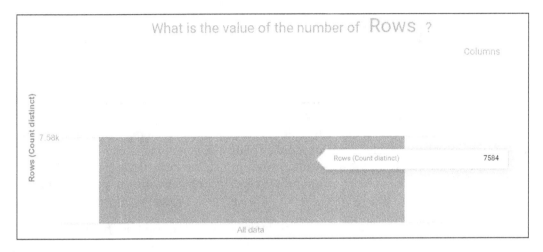

Notice that if you move your mouse over the visualization, you see an exact row count, that is, **7584**.

Now I want to add more content to my visualization, so I click on **Columns** in the top-right corner of the page, as shown in the following screenshot, and then click on **Add a column**:

From there, I select the **crimedescr** field column (highlighted in the next image).
Then I click on **Done**:

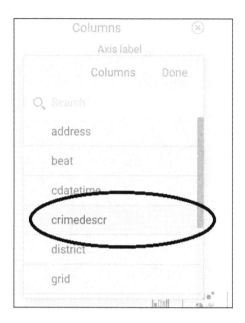

Now Watson Analytics adds the *breakdown by (crime) description*:

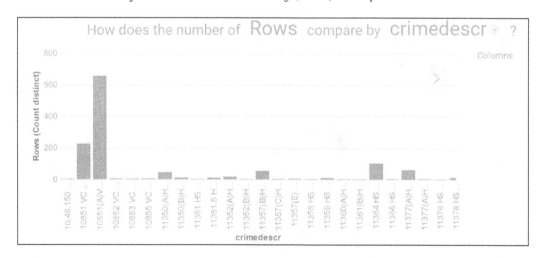

This is a bit more interesting, but let's see a breakdown of *only those crimes considered petty*. To do that, click on **Columns** again and then click on **crimedescr**. You'll see that everything is selected—meaning *all crimes* are included in the visualization:

Let's click on **Set a condition** and then type the word `petty` under **Contains**, as shown here:

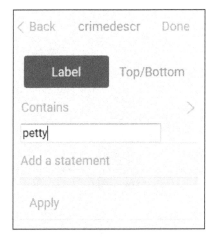

Finally, let's click on **Apply**. IBM Watson Analytics now rebuilds our visualization, showing only crimes with the word **petty** in their description:

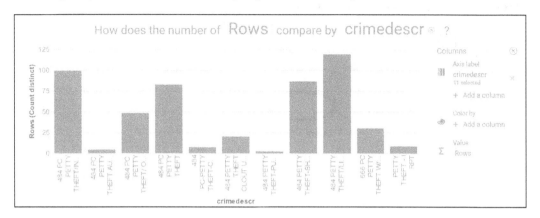

Context

Keep in mind that sometimes Watson Analytics needs help. For example, Watson Analytics provided us with the following visualization: **How do the values of grid compare by beat?**

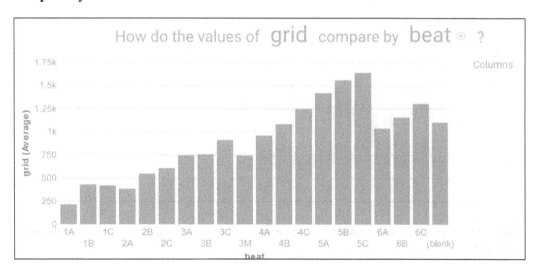

It's a nice-looking visualization, but the problem is that it is meaningless, since Watson Analytics is interpreting the *value* of the **grid** field as **amount** or **total** when I know that it's really a *numeric identifier* (of a unique grid).

A more reasonable visualization may be generated (using this visualization as a starting point) if we click on the word **grid** and select a different field (perhaps **Rows**), as shown in this screenshot:

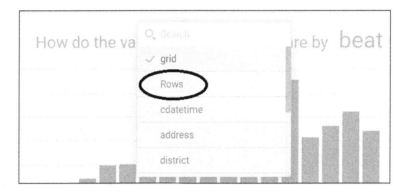

Now, Watson Analytics shows us a visualization of **Rows** by **beat** (meaning the number of crimes occurring in each city beat):

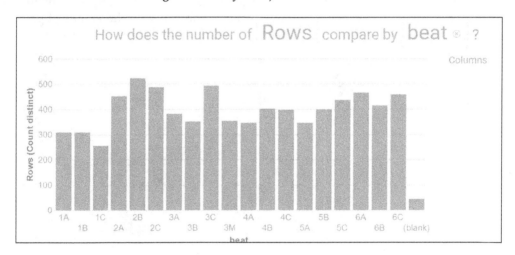

The key is to use visualizations as *starting points* for the development of insights into your data—question everything!

Sharing an insight

Now might be a good time to introduce a nice feature of Watson Analytics—*sharing*.

Let's say your *continued exploration* of the crime file has yielded the visualization shown in the next screenshot—the total number of crimes by grid: **How do the values of grid compare by district?** Excited about what you see, you want to share with others how the districts are doing:

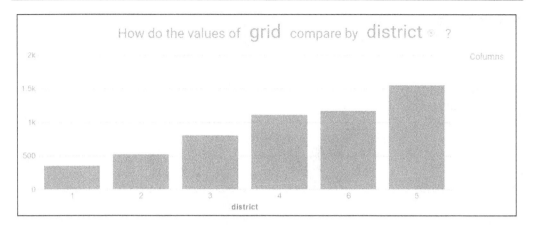

In the top-left corner on the page of Watson Analytics, notice the *share* icon (shown circled here):

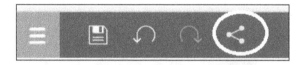

Clicking on the share icon opens the **Share** dialog:

From this dialog, you can choose your method of communication: **Email** (based on your Watson Analytics account's e-mail), **Download** (as an image, PDF, or PowerPoint presentation), through **Social Media** (Twitter, Facebook, or LinkedIn) or as a **Link** (which you can forward to other Watson Analytics users). This is an easy way to share your insights or solicit additional input from your associates.

Saving your work

Of course, once you have found something you want to keep, you should save it.

Typically, there are two options: **Save** and **Save As**. Watson Analytics supports both. In this screenshot, you can see (circled and from left to right) the **Save As** icon and the **Save** icon:

Predictions (discussed in a later chapter of this book) are *automatically* saved when you create or change them. Explorations, views, and refined datasets (for all of these, we have shown many examples) must be *manually* saved by using **Save** or **Save As**.

Once you've begun saving your explorations, you can reopen them by clicking on the **Collection** icon, as shown in the following screenshot, and selecting from the list that appears:

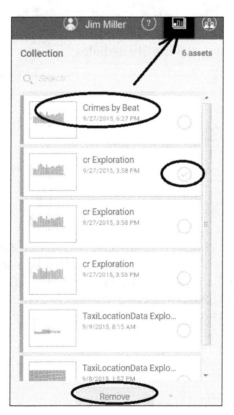

Summary

In this chapter, we discussed the process and importance of developing a proper use case, how it relates to Watson Analytics, and — specifically — how a use case may correspond to questioning your data, as well as the vitally important point of establishing the context of your data. We explained how to create questions in Watson Analytics and how Watson Analytics interprets and processes them. Finally, example use cases were offered for the purpose of clarification.

In the next chapter, we will cover the importance of Watson solution design and what needs to be considered before starting a project, from the overall design of a content analytics solution to the expectations from the resulting analysis.

3

Designing Solutions with Watson Analytics

Although simple *explorations*, like the examples in the previous chapter can provide you with keen insights, on the long term, your organization will require a more comprehensive Watson Analytics *analytical solution approach* to be developed.

In this chapter, we will cover the process of taking a *sound approach* to leveraging IBM Watson Analytics for content analytics, what to think about before you start, how to develop an *end-to-end solution design*, and how to set your *expectations for the resulting analysis*.

This chapter is organized as follows:

- Data considerations
- Best practices to build a content analytics collection
- Watson Analytics' programming interfaces

Data considerations

Understanding your data and its characteristics is important—but before focusing on data, it's a good idea to have at least a high-level understanding of what the Content Analytics data model is, since it is what Watson Analytics is founded on.

The Content Analytics data model

The data model's *foundation* is a *collection*—or a *content analytics collection*. This collection starts with one or more documents *crawled* from one or more content sources. A *logical document* is then created from the *original document (or documents)*.

The original sourced or *crawled* document is the main content that is used to create the logical document, along with any additional information inserted into the document during the *document processing phase* described in *Chapter 2, Identifying Use Cases*. Logical documents are made up of *fields* and *facets*, and you can have only a single logical document per collection. Imagine fields as **indexes** and facets as different **views** of the document (or documents) in the collection. Finally, a *content analytics miner* is a tool used to *mine* the collection, with facets presented in **Facet Navigation pane** of the content analytics miner and fields shown with each document search result in the middle of the content analytics miner window.

A relational mindset

Look at the next diagram. Using the *relational database* concept, you might think of the content analytics model described previously by equating the *crawled source document* with its main content as a *raw database table* that has been loaded with transactions from perhaps multiple sources. A process has then created indexed **logical views** of that raw table based on its data and various relevant business rules. This may be similar to the logical document. Finally, a query tool is available to query or *mine* that content (information):

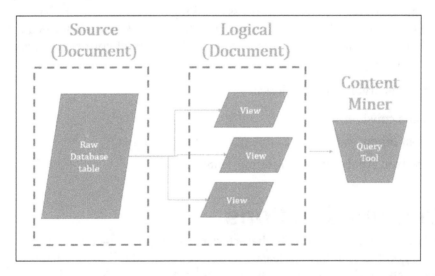

Using the preceding relational database model, you may better understand if you imagine a content analytics collection as an actual relational database consisting of many raw data tables (or documents) processed into indexed and optimized views that make up a logical view (or document). This document can be mined with a query tool that understands the different views, fields, and indexes.

Okay, now that you understand what the content analytics data model is, don't worry. It is completely *hidden* from you when you are using Watson Analytics! Watson Analytics *simply leverages the technology* (using the cloud to make it practically available instantly, anywhere in the world) to enhance, scale, and accelerate human expertise.

Structured and unstructured sources

Typically, a relational database will support a large number of associations that can be defined for the data it contains. We would consider a relational database to be considered a *highly structured* data source, although it may contain text in the VCHAR, CLOB, or BLOB fields.

Since Content Analytics supports many types of data sources, the level at which the data is structured will vary greatly from data source to data source. This dictates that you should carefully consider whether the data you will use lacks structure when designing a content analytics approach or solution.

A reminder

If you are still using the free edition of Watson Analytics and you want to include data from sources such as a relational database, you'll need to extract data from the database and upload it to Watson Analytics as a file. You can upgrade to the personal or professional editions to connect directly to data sources such as the IBM SQL or Bluemix.

Data categorized

The three categories of the data are shown in the following figure:

Little or No Structure	No Structure & Structured	Highly Structured

You'll find that data sources fall under one of these three categories:

- Sources with *little or no structure* in the data (simple text files)
- Sources containing *both structured and unstructured* data (data pulled from document management systems)
- Sources containing *highly structured* data (such as our relational database example)

How your data source is categorized will determine how you prepare and work with your data. Potentially, you may be able to leverage the text analytics power available in *Content Analytics to find and extract insights,* or you may already have structured fields in your data from which value can be extracted. Other than this, you may need to preprocess your data with another tool.

At the time of writing this book, Watson Analytics does not analyze unstructured data without it being *preprocessed.* To use Watson Analytics with data that is highly unstructured, you must use an external tool (such as SPSS modeler) along with Watson Analytics' explore and redefine features. You have to do this to *structuralize* your data source for analysis.

Multiple data sources

For a given Content Analytics collection, you have the option of defining multiple *crawlers* to source data. Typically, a single crawler is defined for each source data type. To configure a crawler, you *match up* the fields in your source to the index fields in your content analytics collection.

 If you are working with only one data source and using only a single crawler, *matching up* the fields (as just mentioned) is less complicated. For multiple sources and different crawlers, this is not the case, and it can be a complicated task.

In Watson Analytics, there are no configurable *crawlers.* In fact *you* are the crawler! That is to say that you (as we described in an earlier chapter) create a file from your data source (or sources) and upload it to Watson Analytics for analysis. If you want to use data residing in multiple data sources, you have to manually create and combine the files before you upload them. Many modeling tools (and programmer editors as well), such as IBM SPSS modeler, make this task much easier (although it would have been nice if Watson Analytics supported this).

Of course, Watson Analytics does support *replacing data in a dataset*. Potentially, if data from multiple sources has the same format (and characteristics), you can update a dataset that is already uploaded to Watson Analytics. Remember, however, that when you replace the data in a dataset, the predictions, explorations, and views that are based on that dataset are updated. To replace a data file, click on the file in Watson Analytics and select **Replace all data**, as shown in this screenshot:

Date-sensitive data

You may think of a discoverable *insight* in terms of a pattern or trend you find in your data that occurs over a specific period of time. For Content Analytics to accomplish this, it must have one or more dates occurring consistently in the collection that it is examining. Without that date (or dates), it is not possible to perform calculations such as time series, deviations, and trend views, all which depend upon a date.

Working with dates can be difficult, especially when working with data from multiple data sources. Again, Watson Analytics does not currently provide much help and better off manipulating your dates before uploading them to Watson Analytics.

Watson Analytics does grant the ability to change *some* field data types (to `Number`, `Text`, `Date`, or `Time` interval) by clicking on the field/column, then clicking on the more icon ⋮ , and finally selecting **Properties**. However, Watson Analytics does not provide an easy way to reformat a date field. Again, this is best done outside of Watson Analytics (before uploading the data).

Another possible way (which is supported) to deal with dates in Watson Analytics is by *grouping data* — you could, perhaps, group a date field formatted as MM/DD/YYYY by month or year to make it easier to analyze.

Extracting information from textual data

Once again, Content Analytics provides accessing and analyzing text from data sources by using what are referred to as *annotators*. Annotators provide the ability to look through textual data and match words, phrases, or even synonyms. In addition, annotators attempt to find patterns (based on rules that you set up).

And once again, Watson Analytics isn't that capable. Certainly, textual fields (columns) can be included as part of an uploaded data file, but *out of the box*, Watson Analytics treats those fields as unique values. We can set up filters, for example (like the previous chapter's example that limited visualization by including only records with a particular word in the field).

The following is a visualization of a comparison of crimes (crime description) by grid, with a filter applied to *only include crimes with the word "vehicle" in their description*:

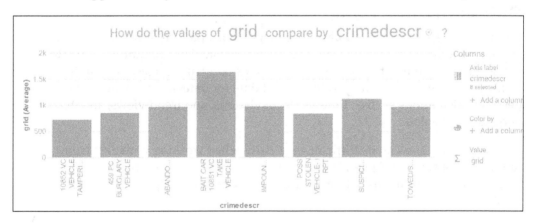

Other kinds of data, such as *machine logs* or *e-mails*, do not work well with Watson Analytics at this point in time, unless significantly preprocessed before being uploaded.

Multiple collections

With Content Analytics, you can create multiple (Content Analytics) collections, with each consisting of specific crawlers, Content Analytics, and indexing. This is most advantageous to perform research projects that are independent and unique in nature. In fact, you can even *group collections* by an administrator-assigned application ID so that security and other business rules can be assigned.

In Watson Analytics, collections are a bit different; they are simply a way of *holding on to* artifacts or *assets* that you have (or Watson Analytics has) created or accumulated along the way. For example, as you work with Watson Analytics, you can *set aside* interesting or important visualizations from **Explore**, **Predict**, and **Assemble**. In **Assemble**, you can also set aside other objects, such as images. You can then add these visualizations and items to dashboards and stories that you create later.

To view your collection (or list of saved items) in Watson Analytics, click on the **Collection** icon in the top-right corner of the welcome or main page (shown next), and click on the icon again to hide the collection list:

Of course, you can add visualizations, for example, to a collection list, by clicking on the collect icon in the bottom-right corner of the page while viewing a visualization. This icon is encircled here:

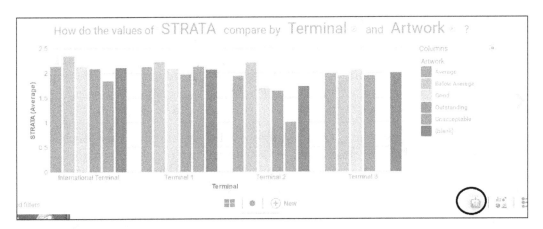

Building collections

A Content Analytics collection is key to the process of finding insights in an *efficient manner*, as it supports the ability to quickly search and discover. Your collections should be comprised from *your data*. This is the data extracted from areas within your organization—preferably multiple data sources. Use data from relational databases, filesystems, document management sources, the Web, and so on.

With Watson Analytics, the idea of *a collection* is more on the lines of *ongoing collecting*. That is, as you progress and become more familiar with how Watson Analytics works, you will *collect* (or *save a copy* of) *artifacts* from **Explore**, **Predict**, and **Assemble**, so that you can then *reuse* them in new visualizations, dashboards, and stories.

The collection process – step by step

We just showed how you can add a *visualization* to a *collection*. Let's now take a look at the Watson Analytics **Predict** and **Assemble** features.

By using *Explore*, you use the power of Watson Analytics to explore and visualize your data. To *analyze* your data, you create a *prediction* from data that you have already uploaded to the Watson Analytics environment. A Watson Analytics prediction identifies the data that you are analyzing and includes visual and text insights that are generated from the data.

To create a Watson Analytics prediction, go to the Watson Analytics welcome page, click on *Add*, and then click on **Predict** (next, upload or choose existing data). Alternatively, you can click on a dataset that you have already uploaded to Watson Analytics and then click on **Predict**.

On the **Create a new analysis** page (shown next), type a name (to name your prediction) in the **Name your workbook** field:

Now you need to evaluate your targets. Targets are fields that are influenced by other fields in the data. The **Predict** capability defines the default targets and field properties.

For this example, I'm using one of our previous data files, SlotsResults, and perhaps I'm interested in the **Weekday** field to find out what might influence (or drive) a weekday's results. A key driver is a field or a combination of fields that has a statistically significant effect on a target field.

Watson Analytics has selected **Type** as a target field for us. If I don't want to select **Type**, I can click on **X** to the right of it to delete it, as follows:

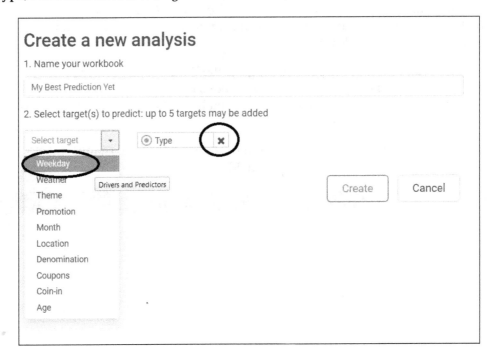

Once you click on **Create**, Watson Analytics starts working on your prediction:

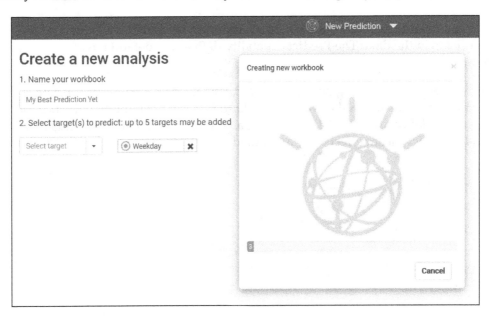

A message (shown in the preceding screenshot) provides you with an idea of the progress as Watson Analytics creates your prediction. When the prediction completes, you can view the summary for it and explore the output in detail.

Watson Analytics has created this prediction:

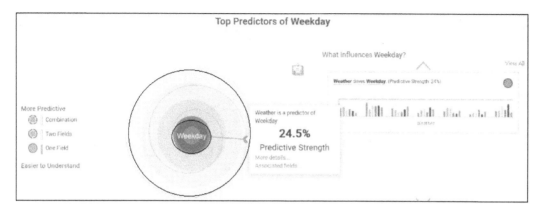

If you move your mouse over the solid dot connected to **Weekday** in the target (as shown in the preceding image), you will see that Watson Analytics has found that **Weather is a predictor of Weekday** (see the next image). From there, you can click on **More details…**:

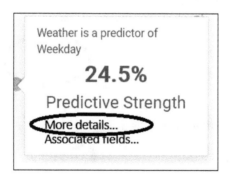

Clicking on **More details…** shows us a nice visualization of **Main Insight** that Watson Analytics has found in our data. You can see that **distribution of Weekday** is shown for each category of **Weather**, as follows:

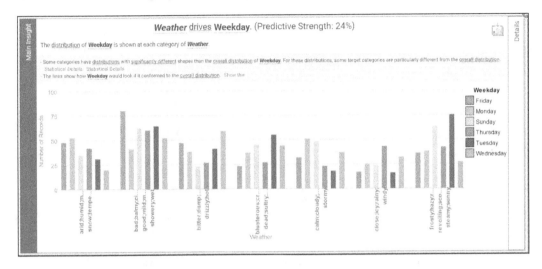

Watson Analytics has provided us with many more details regarding this insight, such as Weathers **Predictive Strength**, but for now, let's save this information in our collection. To do that, we simply click on the collect icon in the top-right corner:

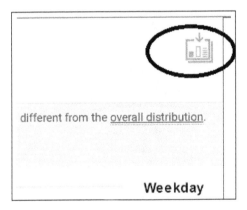

After clicking on **Collect**, this is what we see:

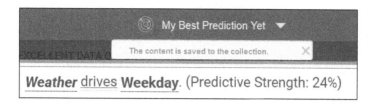

Now we have this insight *saved* in our *collection*, and so it is easily accessible by us in the future.

Adding to collections from assemble

So we've seen *explorations* and *predictions*. Now let's look at Watson Analytics' **Assemble** feature. With **Assemble**, you can create unique and exciting *views* to express the analysis and insights that you discovered in **Predict** and **Explore**. You create these views with new visualizations or *artifacts* that you previously added to your collection, which includes saved visualizations and various other sources such as text, media, web pages, images, and shapes. Let's walk through an example.

Just like creating a new prediction, you can go to the **Welcome** page and click on **Add**. Then select an existing data file, add a new data file (to the Watson Analytics environment), or click on **Skip**:

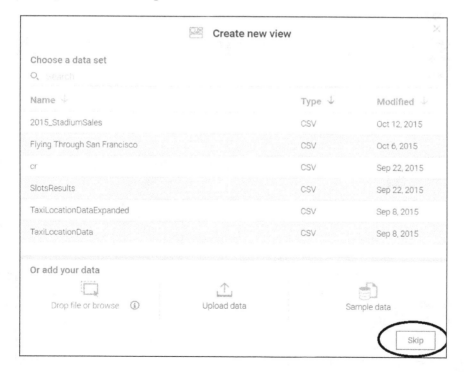

For this example, let's click on **Skip**, and when Watson Analytics shows us **Create a View page**, we can type a name for our new view in the **Name your view** textbox, as shown here:

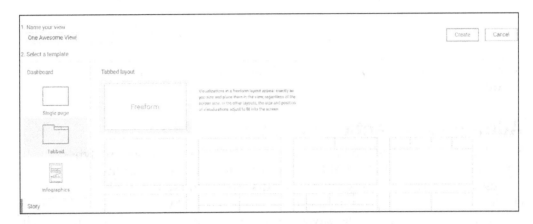

The next step would be to select a template from the left-hand side of the page. A template provides a *format* or *layout* for your **View** page. This is similar to Microsoft's PowerPoint slide layouts.

There are several choices, but for now, let's keep it simple and go to **Dashboard | Single page**:

For our single view page, we can still select from several different *styles* based on what we are intending to create (or *assemble*) from our collected artifacts (or as Watson Analytics refers to them, *assets*). I'll choose the type that includes two *sections* — an upper banner area and a main area:

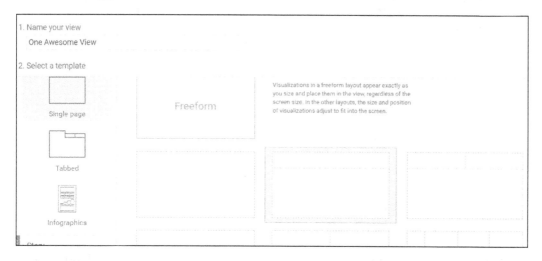

Now, we can click on the **Collection** icon (shown next) to scroll through everything we've saved up to this point:

At the top of our collection list, we can see the **Prediction** we saved earlier in this chapter (named **My Best Prediction Yet**). We can click on it and *drag it* into our view. Be sure to *drop it* on the *lower content panel* and center it:

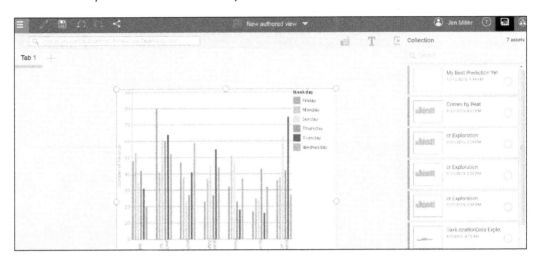

Let's also add a little more to our view page. In the top-right corner, you'll notice an icon bar:

These icons allow you to add visualizations, text, media clips, web pages, images, and shapes to your view page. Each can be added in a similar way: by clicking on the icon and making a selection or providing a URL or address. Watson Analytics also allows you to change your view page's **Theme** and **General style** (color). As you add to your view page, each of the selections can also be saved, or "collected" as an artifact or asset. Let's walk through some examples.

To add a visualization, I click on the **Visualizations** icon. From there, I think I'd like to add a **Word Cloud** to my view page, so I will click on the word cloud icon:

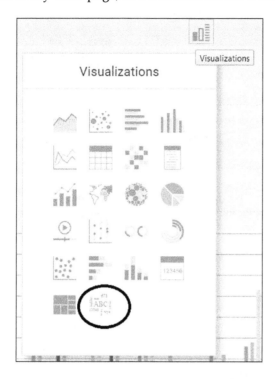

Watson Analytics adds a **Word Cloud** and waits for me to customize it:

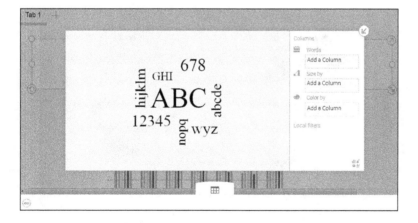

Notice the **Data Tray** at the bottom of your view page. This is where you can select fields from any data file that you may have loaded into the Watson Analytics environment to customize your **Word Cloud**:

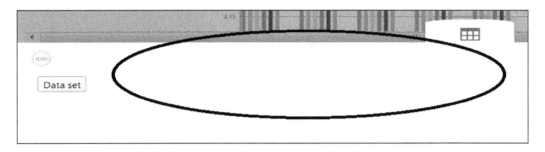

If no fields are visible in the data tray, click on the **Data set** icon to the left of the tray (shown in the preceding image). This will allow you to scroll through and select a dataset to display:

I'll select the file we are working with in this example (that is, **SlotsResults**), and Watson Analytics will show me the list of fields in the file:

Now I can click to select a field from the list (shown in the preceding screenshot) and *drag the field* into the word cloud **Words** textbox (to the right of my word cloud). Once I have done that, Watson Analytics populates the data tray for me:

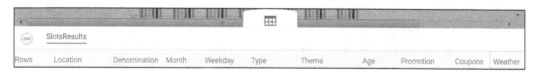

Using the now-populated data tray, I can select and drag more fields onto my word cloud, so I now have **Words**, **Size by**, and **Color by** populated. Watson Analytics can now build my word cloud:

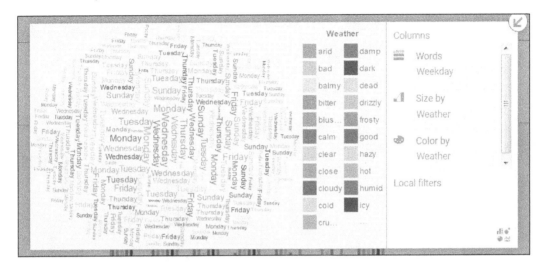

Once I've added my word cloud to my view page, I can always click on it to revise it, using the Watson Analytics-displayed *edit icon bar* above it:

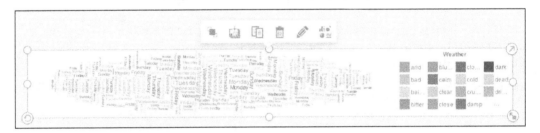

From the edit icon bar, you can do these actions: **ReOrder**, **Collect**, **Duplicate**, **Trash**, (**Edit the title**, or **Change the visualization**. Let's add a title.

Click on the title icon and simply *type the text you want* to add:

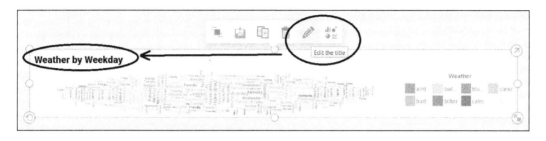

Before we go any further, let's give our view page the same name. Simply click on the **Save** icon in the top-left corner of your view page:

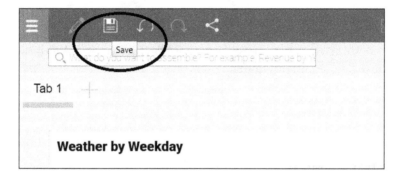

In the **Save As** popup, type the name to save the view page as Weather by Weekday, and then click on **Save**, as shown here:

Now, since we've done the work required to create our interesting word cloud, let's *collect it* (save it as part of our artifact or asset list). To do this, just click on the **Collect** icon:

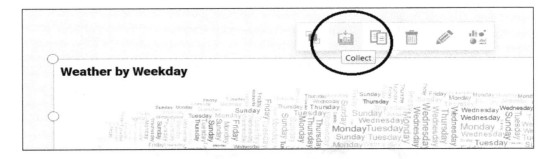

Now, if we check our asset list, we will see that **Weather by Weekday** is saved and available for future use, as shown here:

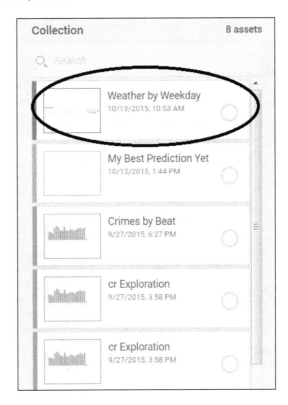

An interesting behavior when you save assets from a view page is that each is saved under the view page name (rather than an individual asset name). As an example, let's add an image to our view page.

Again, we go back to our *edit icon bar*, click on the **Image** icon, and provide a location for the image:

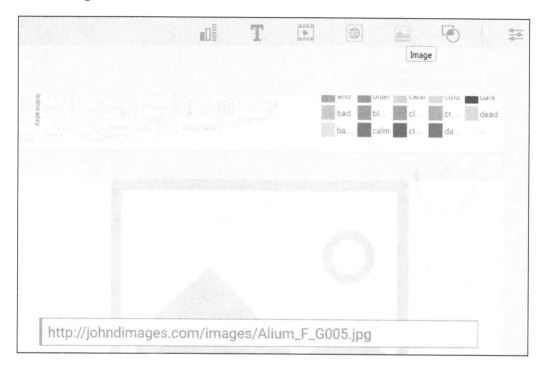

Our image is now visible on our view page, next to our original visualization (as shown in the next screenshot). So let's click on it and again select **Collect**:

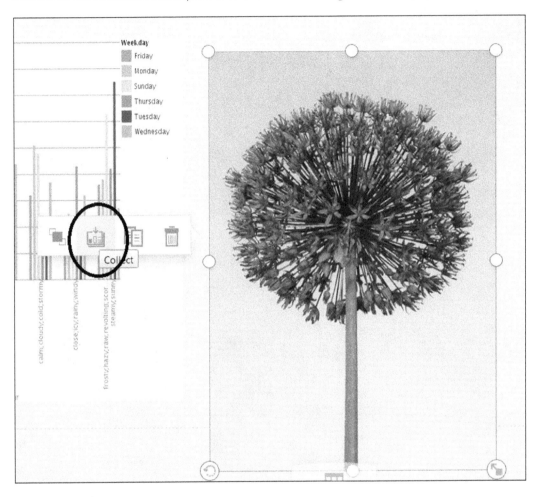

If you check your collection now, you will see that Watson Analytics has added two assets, both named **Weather by Weekday**, but both only contain the item selected and saved (in this case, the word cloud and the image):

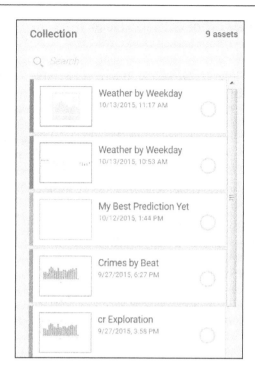

A helpful hint

When building your *content analytics collection*, take time to first determine what makes sense to *keep around* and how that asset or artifact should be *named* for later identification and use. Remember that, when it comes to organizing a Watson Analytics collection, we have only **Add**, **Remove**, and **Search**, so a long list of vaguely identified assets in a collection will be less helpful than you might expect.

Planning for iteration

A generally accepted best-practice approach to creating a Watson Analytics *solution* (also perhaps referred to as an assembled dashboard, or story) or analytical collection is through *iteration*. What this means is starting with a smaller file of *sample data* so that you can quickly validate the design you are thinking of (before proceeding to a full set of data).

Depending on the source of your data, the data may be anywhere from hundreds of records (rows) to tens of thousands of records (and beyond) in size. The more the records (data) that you use, the longer it takes to upload to the Watson Analytics environment (and consequently, it will take longer to parse, analyze, and build your collections). It is advisable to first select a file with a number of records that is *reasonable* for your needs to get started effectively.

By starting with a *smaller sized file*, you'll find it easier to do things (in addition to simply uploading the file to Watson Analytics) such as refining and formatting the data, creating and saving assets, and so on. A word of caution here: with fewer records, you'll *not get meaningful statistics* or valid insights (although they may still be interesting!). However, the objective is to refine the process of exploring and refining the data first, and then proceed with additional iterations of versions of the file with increasing size of the file by a certain percentage each time. Of course, with larger datasets, you'll have more opportunities to find specific entities and patterns in the data that you may be looking for.

So to the point, the *best practice* advice is to do your designing iteratively with a *small* record collection at first and with multiple iterations following (each time increasing the size of the data used).

Programming interfaces

The formal *IBM Content Analytics platform* provides numerous **Application Programming Interfaces** (**APIs**) from which you can create search, analytics, and administration applications; modify crawled documents; filter search results; export documents; set up an identity management component to enforce document-level security; and perform ad hoc text analysis on documents.

These programming interfaces include:

- REST APIs
- IBM search and index APIs
- Plugin APIs
- Identity management component APIs
- Real-time **natural language processing** (**NLP**) APIs

The idea of *programming* with Watson Analytics is a bit different.

Programming with Watson Analytics

With Watson Analytics, there is really no structured programming involved. The Watson Analytics interface does allow you to *create* solutions or *views* — using the **Assemble** feature for example — for reuse by yourself and others. These views can be either *dashboards* (we created one earlier in this chapter) or *stories*. A story is just another style of view, but one that contains a *number of "views"* that are displayed in order over a set period of time.

Stories are really pretty close to a dashboard in that you choose assets you created with **Explore** and **Predict**, but also provide an account of those assets over a span of time and attempt to drive a conclusion or make a recommendation.

Rather than *programming*, Watson Analytics provides you with the ability to simply and easily:

- Explore and refine the information you have
- Make predictions using the results of your explorations and refinements
- Assemble artifacts from your explorations and predictions into a *presentation*

Summary

In this chapter, we pointed out specific data considerations to be aware of before uploading data to the IBM Watson Analytics environment. In addition, we introduced the concept of a *content analytics collection* and *what it means in Watson Analytics*. Finally, we spoke about what *programming* is available within the Watson Analytics interface.

In the next chapter, we will discuss the *process of* content analysis and how you can use IBM Watson Analytics to help analyze big data.

4
Understanding Content Analysis

In this chapter, we will talk about the practice of *content analysis* and how IBM Watson Analytics can be used as a tool to help analyze big data.

This chapter is organized in the following way:

- Basic concepts of Content Analytics
- Cycle of analysis with Content Analytics using Watson Analytics
- An illustrative use case

Basic concepts of Content Analytics

Content Analytics focuses on *textual data* that is typically difficult to analyze. Because of its unformatted and ambiguous nature, potential insights hidden within this data are often never realized. Generally, using commonly-known automated methods (to understand this type of data) is at best, difficult. This leaves a potentially large *body of opportunity* not considered when making key decisions. Previously, attempts to include this data in decision making were dependent upon great manual efforts.

For example, by *reading customer satisfaction surveys one by one*, an organization may gain an understanding of what individual customers are thinking, but may not know *if satisfied customers are unique cases or common cases, or if such cases are increasing or decreasing*. This kind of understanding can be acquired *only by analyzing the data set as a whole*. However, textual data will generally contain huge varieties of information – some valuable and some not - making it important to focus on only the valuable information.

Content Analytics is designed to help with this. It allows *efficient analysis* of *entire data sets* to find *patterns and trends*, and supports the identification of those particular patterns and trends that are important to you. This allows you to reach greater levels of awareness and achievement with your data.

Manual or automation

We shouldn't have to take too much time to convince you that trying to manually evaluate significant amounts of textual data is problematic and expensive.

The generally accepted process of analyzing data consists of:

- Classifying the data into groups with predefined characteristics (also known as *setting the objectives* for the analysis)
- Totaling the numbers found that fit each group
- Presenting the totals

This sounds simple, but problems occur:

- The amount of data becomes large
- Data is ambiguous and isn't easily classified into a predefined group

During manual analysis (of textual data), analysts usually randomly select a more manageable (but perhaps not an actual representation) subset of the data and can potentially misclassify data into groups, based upon ambiguous understandings.

The idea of using Content Analytics is to use an automated means to analyze your textual data, easily processing thousands more records than a manual process ever could. The objective is to change the analyst from a *document classifier and chart maker* to an *interpreter of the analytical results*.

Difficulties with textual analysis

Since textual data is, in fact, *text* or words and phrases written for and intended for humans rather machines, it is challenging for automated processing to always correctly interpret it. For example:

- A phrase can be interpreted in different ways
- Some words can be both an adjective or a noun
- Words may have different meanings, such as a name of a person or place
- Words could be used as *past tenses* or as *an object*

- Some key words in a phrase may affect the overall meaning of the phrase
- Words and concepts may often be overly ambiguous
- Misspellings often result in ambiguity
- Order or timeliness may change the acceptable meaning of a term

You can see that the preceding challenges (and others) might cause the analytical results to not always match with your expectations.

Humans performing manual analysis are the best way to improve on the accuracy of your text analytic process, but it is impractical as the volume of your textural data increases. One might suggest adding more people to the process but different people (in fact, even the same analyst) can produce completely different results over time.

The way that Content Analytics works—using definitions and pattern matching rules—makes it a much more productive process than the manual alternative. In addition, it is important to understand that using Content Analytics keeps the criteria for interpretation the same for the entire data set. This allows the analysts to spend more time analyzing results and perhaps taking action based upon the examination of *all* of the data, even large amounts of data, which leads to a higher value result.

Frequency and deviation

Another area where Content Analytics can improve the analytical process and ultimately the results is with dealing with *frequency* and *deviation*.

Frequency is the *number of times* that contain keywords are identified within unique responses or records. *Deviation* refers to the change or changes in responses (or the number of occurrences of those keywords).

Without considering the entire data set and identifying and understanding relationships within the data, the results produced may still not reflect reality.

Again, Watson Analytics Content Analytics ensures a much broader analysis of all of the data to discover new relationships and provide more reliable insights.

Precision and recall

Finally, results based upon large amounts of textual data are dependent on the factors precision (accuracy) and recall (coverage). Precision is defined as the ratio of the correctly returned results versus the total returned results or the number of true positives. Recall is defined as the ratio of the correctly returned results versus the total number of correct results in the data set.

In general, aiming for *higher recall* is more challenging than aiming for *higher precision*. To achieve higher precision, the goal is noise elimination; for higher recall, the idea is to search extensively to be sure to capture all relevant information.

Dealing with precision and recall is common in Content Analytics. Tools like IBM SPSS offer options for preprocessing your data to improve precision and recall. In Watson Analytics, as we mentioned in an earlier chapter, you can use the *Refine* feature to help with this.

Cycle of analysis with Watson Analytics

A high-level look at the *practice of content analysis* reveals five basic steps, or *phases*:

1. Defining a purpose (for the analysis effort)
2. Obtaining relevant data
3. Performing the analysis
4. Determining action(s) to take
5. Validation

Note that you'll utilize Watson Analytics when *performing the analysis* and this step involves a series of *sub-steps*:

1. Applying preprocessing logic to the data, if required.
2. Performing analysis using Watson Analytics.
3. Evaluating starting or entry points.
4. Reapplying preprocessing logic to the data, if appropriate.
5. Repeating the analysis and verifying changes.
6. Reprocessing, modifying logic as necessary.

Defining a purpose

This important step is unrated and typically over looked. The power of Watson Analytics can best serve if you have a purpose in mind (a question to ask or notion to validate) when loading specific data. Watson Analytics documentation says it this way:

What do you think this data can reveal?

Using examples from earlier chapters, you might want to know:

- Does the location of a stadium stand affect sales?
- Does the outcome of a game affect souvenir sales?
- Does the theme of a slot machine affect profits?
- Do promotions affect slot machine profits?
- Is there a particular type of crime that occurs most often?
- What area in the city has the highest crime occurrence?

Before using Watson Analytics, it is a very good idea to:

- Consider multiple objectives and write them down. Some may not be feasible because of a lack of data, but keep in mind that you can always improve the data as you go along.
- Keep in mind that you may not be able to determine if your objectives are reasonable until you perform the actual analysis.

Obtaining the data

In any analysis, the data is critical. This means that for best results—even with Watson Analytics—it's important to review what data you have, the condition of that data and, what data you may need to locate. You will find that it may take several iterations before Watson Analytics provides reasonable insights.

As you go through each iteration, you must strive to understand and *develop* the data—perhaps by gathering supplemental data or performing significant data cleansing.

Performing the analysis

After you have created your list of objectives (your *purpose*) and identified what you think is a *relevant pool of data*, you can start analyzing the data with Watson Analytics. To be sure, you can *jump right in* and just load your data and *see what Watson Analytics has to say*, but you will achieve much better results with a controlled approach.

As mentioned earlier in this section, the analysis process will be *iterative*. Watson Analytics has a lot to say and it's not all (at least initially) actionable. Following a controlled approach, you will analyze, evaluate, refine/develop (your data), and repeat until insightful discoveries are made (hopefully achieving the purpose(s) originally defined).

Determining actions to take

Ultimately, what you'd like to be able to do is take actions that are based upon insights attained during your data (and of course you'd like them to be positive actions) analysis. Using a tool like Watson Analytics allows you as a decision maker to make more insightful decisions since you may more clearly see complex relationships within data—even if the data volumes are particularly large and complex. There is a growing trend for organizations that recognize the value of identifying insights with Watson Analytics and have already incorporated it into their analytical toolset.

Validation

The *final step* in the cycle is *validation*. Here, you will *carefully appraise* the results of any actions taken. This is critical to verify the correctness and quality of your analysis efforts. In most cases, the results of the validation will be input to the next cycle (of analysis), driving perhaps realignment of purpose and/or further development of the data used.

A sample use case

To better understand what a Watson Analytics Content Analytics cycle might be like, let's walk through a user case scenario.

Let's suppose I am engaged by a university in the United States that is interested in the idea of possibly investing unallocated budget resources into developing additional extra-curricular programs for its students. It is also, however, not willing to risk the possibility of negatively affecting its students' academic performance.

The university wonders: if a *broader range of,* or *more cultured*, options (or non-academic activities) are offered and more of the student body becomes involved with these activities, will grade point averages drop, or will the ratio of students graduating change compared to the number enrolled? If so, perhaps the university would allocate the additional resources elsewhere. Thankfully, we have data available to load into Watson Analytics to see if we can gain insight into this decision making process.

Step 1: Define the purpose

As we mentioned earlier in this chapter, the first step would be to explicitly define what we believe our purpose or objective is. This can be something like, *Will more student involvement in activities affect grade point averages or the number of students who ultimately graduate?*

Step 2: Obtaining the data

With our objective or purpose clearly in mind, we can now start obtaining what we think is relevant data. The university has supplied us with a file containing student information from (approximately) the last 10 years—complete with sex, age, home addresses, enrolment dates, credits attempted, credits completed, average GPAs, graduation dates, average credits per semester, and so on. It also includes the number of non-academic activities each student is enrolled in.

This appears to be enough to start our *development of the data*, so let's take a look at what's provided. The goal is to first identify and understand. Looking through the information, I see that there is a large variety of information; some information seems to be relevant to our purpose, other information maybe not. The following fields stood out to me, and so I've made an effort to clarify their meaningfulness (for brevity, I've listed only the fields that I decided were relevant to our purpose). Part of this exercise is to look for missing, incomplete, or otherwise seemingly incorrect data:

- **Enrollment age**: The age of the student upon enrollment/acceptance
- **Sex, Marital status**: Personal details
- **Home state**: Geographical location
- **Major (Primary, Secondary)**: Could be undeclared or blank
- **Enrollment date**: Date of joining
- **Sponsor**: This text field is usually blank
- **Credits attempted**: The number of credits the student enrolled in
- **Credits completed**: The number of credits the student completed successfully
- **Credits dropped**: The number of credits dropped (important to know if they dropped it, or failed to complete it)
- **Current GPA/average GPA**: reports for all credits completed to date
- **FT or PT**: Is the student full time or part time?
- **Athlete**: Is the student an active athlete (any sport). Values active/inactive or blank?

- **Number of sports**: Zero or any other number

- **Intramural participant**: Does the student participate in intramural sports? Only tracked as yes or no

- **Scholarship type**: Academic award by university, privately awarded by a non-university source, none (no scholarship), or blank

- **Number of clubs enrolled in**: The number of non-sport, non intramural activities, but organized clubs the student is a part of

- **Expected grad date**: Calculated by major on enrolment date

- **Class of**: Inferred from expected grad date

- **Actual grad date**: The actual date the student gradated can be blank for active students

- **Employed by university**: Does the student have a job at the university? (Paid, non paid, none)

- **Transferred in**: Did the student transfer in from another university?

- **Transferred out**: Did the student transfer out to another university?

- **RA**: Is or was the student a resident advisor?

- **Comments**: These are free form comments from teachers or faculty members about the student

- **Residence**: Where is the student residing while attending? (Dorm, other university housing, other, commuter)

- **Alumni**: Is the student an alumnus (yes or no)? Did a family member graduate from here?

Step 3: Performing the analysis

A good amount of time can be required for the previous step; at some point, you'll want to move on though and load the data into Watson Analytics. Once it's loaded, you certainty have the option to further develop the data, either using the Watson Analytics redefine feature, or by externally modifying the data and reloading and replacing the file (or as a new file).

So let's load this file.

From the welcome page, select **Add** then upload data (as we did in previous examples):

Now that Watson Analytics has our data, the fun begins. Note that Watson Analytics gave our data a score of 84 and considers it of *high quality*. Remember, the higher the quality of your data, the better Watson Analytics predicts and explores. We've had higher data quality scores in some of the other sample data files in the book, so let's see if we can improve the score of this file.

To do that, let's click on the file panel shown in the preceding screenshot and then select **Refine**:

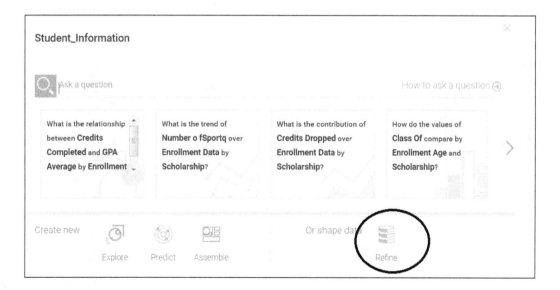

Now, our data is visible in the **Refinement** screen, and we can scroll though the columns and rows and determine what *developments* we may want to make.

First, a bit of *housekeeping*; I noticed one of the column headings contains a typo, so I start thinking ahead to how this data will visualize. Let's clean that up:

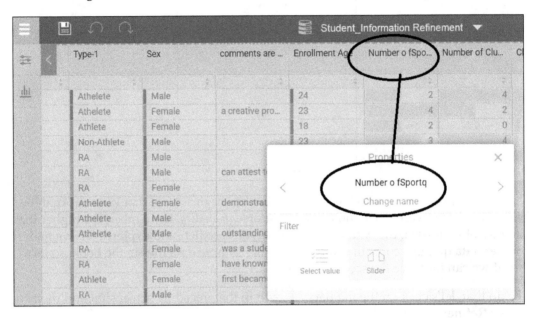

This is better:

One of the more important fields in my file is **GPA Average**. When I click on the heading (see the next screenshot), I see that some records in my file have a blank or missing value for this field. That won't contribute to my analysis well, so I can uncheck the **Include (blank)** to ignore those records:

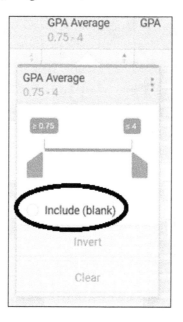

The field **GPA current** has the same dilemma (some blank values), so we can eliminate records with blanks in those fields as well. It is a good practice to identify blank or missing values and consider removing those records or populating those values based upon reasonable assumptions.

Another very important field (based upon our defined purpose) is **Athlete**. We understood that this field would indicate if the student was an *active* athlete (in any sport) and values would be active/inactive or blank. But after clicking on that field heading, we see something different:

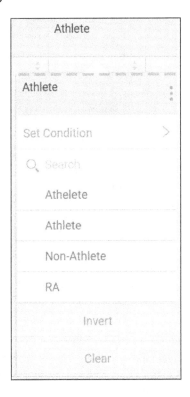

We see that this field actually contains *three* values: **Athlete**, **Non-Athlete**, and **RA**. The concern is, can a student classified as RA also be an athlete?

Whenever possible, you should take the time to validate what you *see in the file* compared to what you *thought should be there*. In this example, suppose we checked with the university and they explained that **RA** indicates that the student was a **Resident Advisor** for other students. Although **RA** is a highly regarded job, it isn't an indication whether the individual was an athlete (or not). With further discussion, we found that the university, as a rule, does not encourage athletes to also be RAs. So it's very rare that a student is both an athlete and an RA. For our needs, we can consider a student RA also a **Non-Athlete**. So that Watson Analytics understands this, we want to transform the field values (change the **RA** to **Non-Athlete**).

[Transformations are rules applied to a field to change values of the field.]

Although Watson Analytics Refine offers certain features like the ability to add calculations and create data groupings to perform filtering, at the time of writing, the easiest method for performing field transformations is external to Watson Analytics using a tool such as IBM SPSS or perhaps even MS Excel (if the volume of your data is small enough).

For our example here, I used MS Excel. Once my transformations were completed, I saved the file with a new name and loaded that file into Watson Analytics. Notice that, even though we've made a few changes to our file, the data quality score did not change:

Now when we look at the field **Athlete,** we see only two values:

We could continue to develop our data, but we can also have a look at what Watson Analytics can expose using the data as it is right now. To do that, we can click on the data panel and select **Explore**. Watson Analytics already prompts us with some starting points (questions), but I have a particular question in mind. I want to see what the average GPA is for athletes and non-athletes. So I can type my question and hit *Enter*:

Watson Analytics rephrases my question a bit into possible visualizations:

Clicking on the first (left to right) question, we see the following visualization:

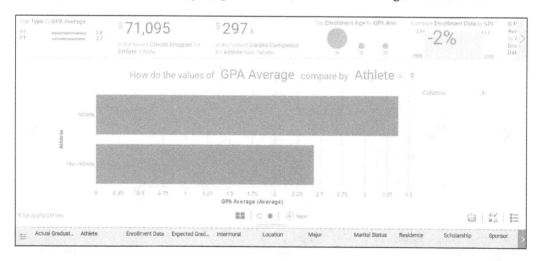

It would *appear* that on average, students who are athletes have accumulated higher GPAs then those students who are non-athletes. However, is that the *full story*? What if we looked at a few other important indicators (for athletes versus non-athletes)? Let's take a look at the *credits completed*.

To do this, we can click on **GPA Average**, and from the drop-down list select **Credits Completed**. Watson Analytics shows us the updated visualization:

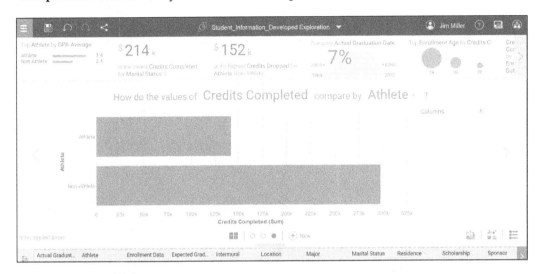

Here, Watson Analytics illustrates that athletes, although they usually have had higher GPAs, have actually *completed fewer credits*. What about *dropped* credits?:

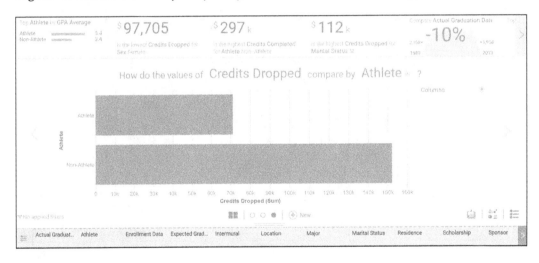

Another question might be *how many credits were attempted?*:

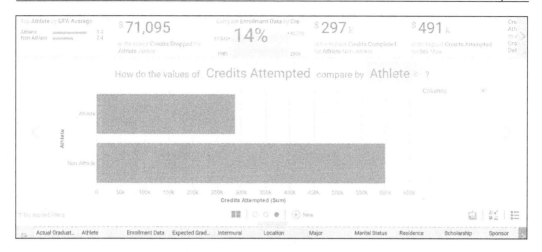

With the preceding Watson Analytics visualizations, we *might* come to understand that non-athletes attempt more credits, complete more credits, but also drop more credits. Athletes seem to perhaps be more *stable* in the number of credits attempted, dropped, and completed—all the while out performing non-athletes from an average GPA perspective. This *insight* might support the proposal originally stated of adding funding to the universities athletic programs.

Step 4: Determining actions to take

Of course, in the preceding example, we completed only superficial development of our data and looked at only a few visualizations (based upon that data) before noticing an insight and drawing a conclusion. Practically speaking, you would perform multiple iterations of steps two (obtaining the data) and three (performing the analysis) before considering any action to take based upon the data.

As you can see, insights need to be validated with others. This may require you to gather more data, or perhaps better understand the data you have (for example, were transformations made actually correct?). In addition, once an insight is validated and a conclusion accepted, don't stop there. For example, if it is eventually accepted that it is a good idea to increase funding for athletic programs (since it appears to positively affect student academic performance), you can ask, "*Is there an even better option for the available funding?*" What about offering more university scholarships? What about funding more clubs?

Let's have a quick look at these two questions with Watson Analytics.

Next, I've asked Watson Analytics, *How do the values of GPA Average compare by Scholarship?* From this visualization, we notice a new data abnormality. The **Scholarship** field includes the value **All Scholarship Types**, which is a *consolidation* of each value—including the value **None**—so it doesn't make sense to include that here:

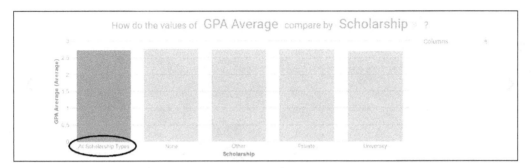

Rather than take the time to cleanse the data (remove this consolidation), we can click on that value and select **Exclude** (shown in the next screenshot):

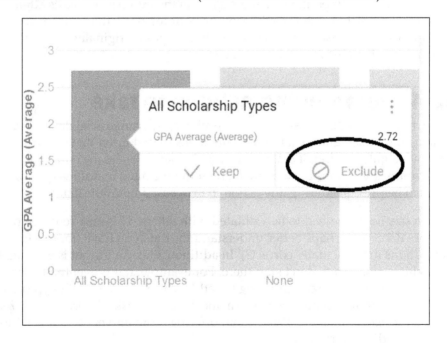

Now, Watson Analytics displays an updated visualization (shown in the next screenshot) that seems to indicate that scholarships don't really affect the average GPA of the student:

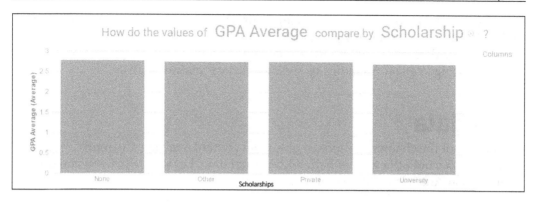

Let's ask Watson Analytics about the effect of club involvement on average GPA, "*How do the values of GPA Average compare by Number of Clubs?*

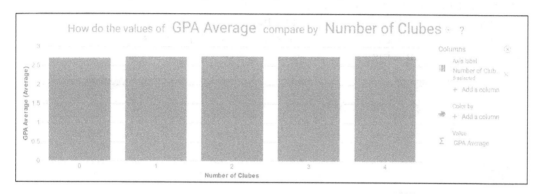

So again, according to the preceding Watson Analytics visualization, it would appear that the *number of clubs* a student is a member of has *no material effect* on the students average GPA.

As you can see, there are numerous patterns of thought that can be explored using Watson Analytics.

Step 5: Validation

Finally, it's been communicated that the validation of any actions taken or decisions made based upon analytical insights is the *final step* in the cycle. In fact, it is absolutely critical to carefully appraise and record the effects of any actions taken. You will find (as we mentioned earlier in this chapter) that the results of this step will be input to the next cycle (of analysis), perhaps driving realignment of purpose and/or further development of the data used.

With each iteration (of the analysis cycle), your data quality scores should improve and the number of useable insights noticed should increase. In my experience, insights drive data development, which in turn drives additional insights. In addition, using Watson Analytics *sharpens* your data analysis skills.

Text data

At the start of the chapter, we looked at textual content analysis. Currently, Watson Analytics does not offer a lot of help with textual data. Let's see what you can do with Watson Analytics and textual data.

Data metrics

Within Watson Analytics Refine, you can click on **Data Metrics** to gain some knowledge of the textual date within your file. In our example (shown in the next screenshot), we see that Watson Analytics scores the **Comments** field as **Low Quality** and provides us a missing values percentage (56 percent):

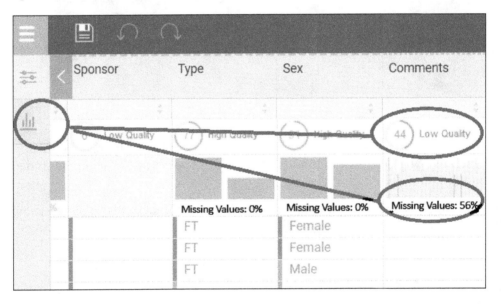

Of course, the field is low quality because not every record in the file has comments (56 percent actually) —a legitimate situation.

Search and Filter

One approach for using Watson Analytics on textual data is perhaps looking for correlations between certain words or phrases found within the data. For example, it might be interesting to see if the presence of the word *leadership* in the comments field has any effect on the GPA average for the university. We can start by formulating a question: *How do the values of GPA Average compare by Comments?*

When Watson Analytics visualizes the answer, we can click on *applied filter* in the lower-left corner of the page:

Then, we can use *search* to find any comments that contain the word we are interested in (leadership), select them, and set them as our filter:

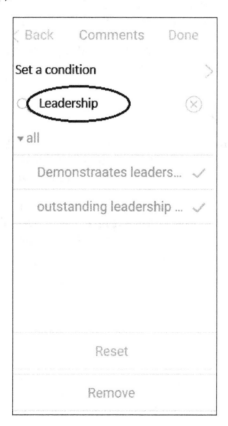

Finally, Watson Analytics shows us our *filtered* visualization:

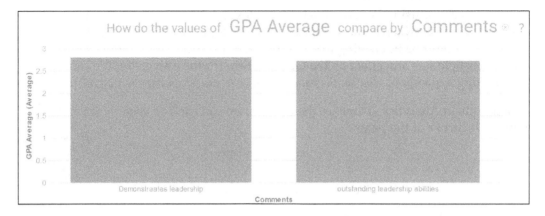

Comments used in our file with the word *leadership* are *demonstrates leadership* and *outstanding leadership abilities* and — according to Watson Analytics — it seems that these students do not have very exciting average GPAs.

The *net* result is that when it comes to textual data, you'll need to perhaps supplement your analysis with preprocessing outside of Watson Analytics.

Summary

In this chapter, we discussed the basic concepts of Content Analytics, as well as the practice or *cycle* of performing a content analytical process. Finally, we used a simple use case example to gain a better understanding of how all this works.

So far, we have focused more on the exploration feature of Watson Analytics. In the next chapter, we will dive deeper into the Predict and Assemble functionalities of Watson Analytics.

5

Watson Analytics Predict and Assemble

In this chapter, we will discuss the Watson Analytics Predict and Assemble functionalities and evaluate a sample use case using these features.

The chapter is organized as follows:

- Predict
- Assemble
- A sample use case

Earlier, we used Watson Analytics Explore to ask questions about several data files and generate interactive visualizations. We used create, filter, and explore to look for patterns and relationships in the data.

In addition to Explore, Watson Analytics also gives us Predict and Assemble. To further analyze a data file, you must create a prediction based on that data. The prediction identifies the data that you are analyzing and includes any insights that are generated from it. Once an insight is identified, you can use the Watson Analytics Assemble capability to express the results of your efforts with Predict and Explore.

Predict

Mining of insights — those previously unknown — from your data typically requires complex modeling using sophisticated algorithms to process the data. With Watson Analytics, however, you *don't have to know* which statistical test to run on your data or even how any of the algorithms actually work.

The method that you use with Watson Analytics is so much simpler; identify/refine your data, create a prediction, and then view the results—*that's it!*

We have already covered identifying and refining data, so let's now look at predictions and how we can *create* a prediction.

First, think of predictions as your *virtual folders* for each predictive analysis effort that you are working on. Here, you identify your data, specify field properties within the data, and select *targets and inputs*. After you've created the prediction, you can view it to see the output of the analysis. The output consists of visual and text insights.

Creating a Watson Analytics prediction

The steps for creating a Watson Analytics prediction are straightforward:

1. Starting on the **Welcome** page, you click on **Predict** (check out the following screenshot):

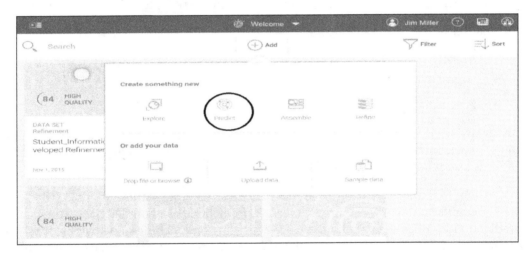

2. Next, on the **Create new prediction** dialog, you select a previously uploaded dataset from the list (or upload new data) that you want Watson Analytics to analyze:

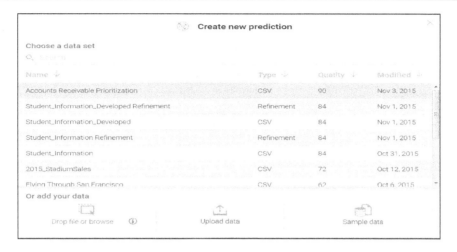

3. On the **Create a new analysis page** (shown in the next screenshot), we set some attributes for our prediction by:

  ° **Giving it a name**: We do this by entering it in the **Name your workbook** field.

  ° **Setting targets**: Targets are the fields that you may be most interested in and want to know more about. These are the fields that are perhaps *influenced by other fields in the data*. When creating a new prediction, Watson Analytics defines default targets and field properties for you, which you can remove (by clicking on the delete icon next to it), and then you can add your own choices (by clicking on **Select target**). Keep in mind that all predictions must have at least one target (and up to five):

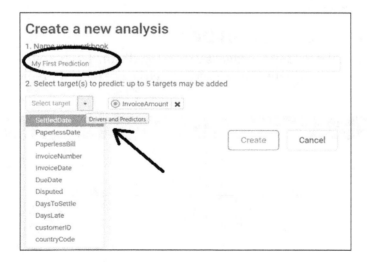

4. Finally, click on **Create**.

Once you have clicked on **Create**, Watson Analytics will generate the prediction.

The following screenshot shows a prediction generated based on a Watson Analytics sample dataset:

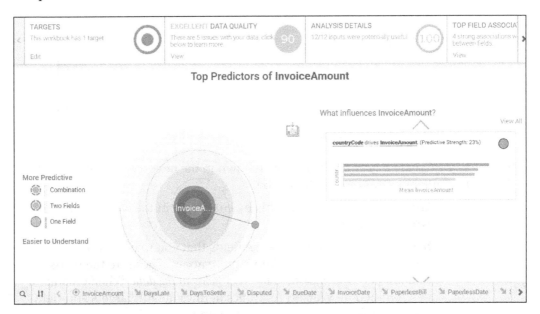

Viewing the results of a prediction

Once a Watson Analytics *prediction* has been generated, you can *view its results*.

Predictor visualization bar

Across the top of the prediction page is the top predictors bar (shown in the following screenshot), where you can click **to select** a particular predictor that is interesting to you:

Main Insights

On the **Main Insight** section of the prediction page (shown in the next screenshot for our example), you can *examine* the *top insights* that Watson Analytics was able to derive from the data:

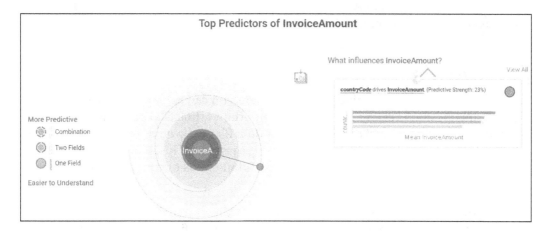

Details

From the **Main Insights** section, you can access (by clicking on the top predictor found — shown circled in the following screenshot) the **Details** page, which gives you the ability to *drill into* the details for the individual fields and interactions of your prediction:

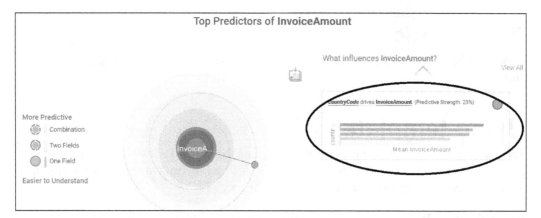

Customization

After you view the results, you might want to *customize* the prediction, to refine the analysis in order to produce additional insights. IBM Watson Analytics allows you to change the number of targets and see the effect of the change on the prediction results. In addition, Watson Analytics allows you to save your updated prediction or revert at any time to any particular version, as desired.

Assemble

The Watson Analytics Assemble feature is where you can actually organize, or *assemble*, the most interesting or otherwise important artifacts exposed while using Watson Analytics to Predict or Explore your data files (as well as other items *collected* or otherwise *set aside* during previous assemble sessions). This, in a way, is where you can do some *programming* to create powerful methods of conveying information to others.

Watson Analytics breaks *assembly* into two types: **Views** and **Dashboards**. Both of these are made up of visualizations (visualizations are defined as a graph, chart, plot, table, map, or any other visual representation of data).

Views

Views are *customizable containers* for dashboards (defined next) and stories (a *set of views* over time).

Dashboards

Dashboards are a specific *type* of view used to help monitor events or activities *at a glance*.

Using templates

To make it easier to assemble your views and dashboards, Watson Analytics provides you with *templates*. They contain predefined layouts and grid lines, for easy arrangement and alignment of visualizations in a view.

As we did with predictions (earlier in this chapter), let's take a look at the **Assemble** process.

From the main or welcome page, click on the plus, or **Add New**, icon (shown in the following screenshot). Then click on **Assemble**:

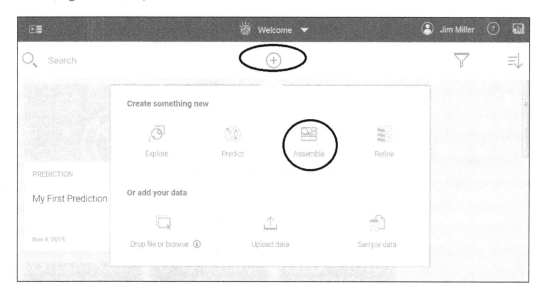

When creating a new assemble, you'll need to *choose a data file* (as shown in the next screenshot) from the list displayed in the **Create new view** dialog (of course, as usual, you can also upload a new file):

Once you select which data file you want to use (simply by clicking on the filename), Watson Analytics shows you the **Create View page**, as shown here:

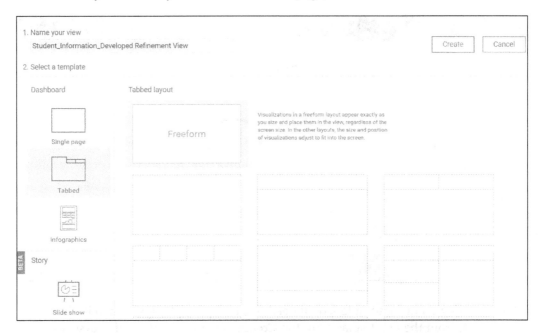

Notice that the **Name your view** field defaults to the name of the file that you selected, and you'll want to change that. Click inside the textbox provided and type an appropriate name for what you are creating, like this:

1. Name your view

    Student Activities

Once you have entered a name for your view, you'll need to decide whether you'd like to assemble a **Dashboard** or a **Story**. Along the *left-hand side* of the page under **Select a template**, you can *scroll vertically* through a list of content types that you can use to organize your visualizations:

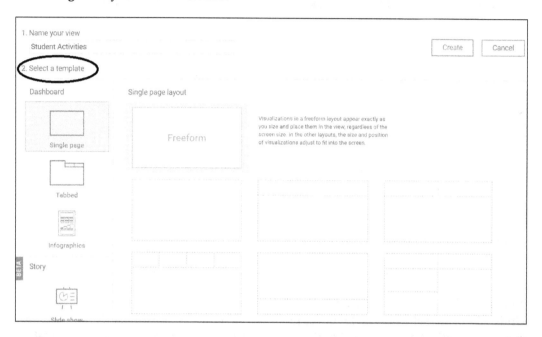

We'll get much deeper into the process of assembling in the next section of this chapter, but for now, let's select **Dashboard** (by clicking on the word **Dashboard**), and then select the **Single Page layout** (by double-clicking on the highlighted rectangle labeled **Freeform**).

Watson Analytics will save your new dashboard and the template will be opened with a blank canvas (shown in this screenshot):

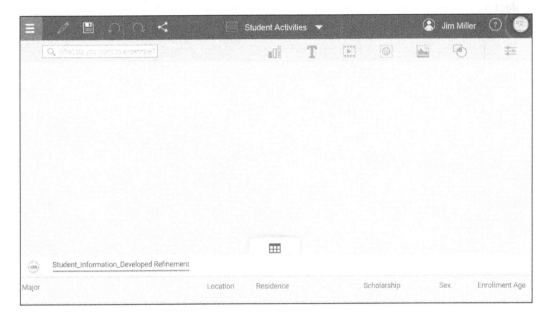

Notice the **Data set** icon (circled in the next screenshot) at the bottom of the canvas. Under the **Data set** icon, the **Data set list** icon, the name of the dataset, and the data columns are displayed. The list of data columns is in what is referred to as the **Data Tray**. If you click on the data set icon, the information below it is hidden. Click on it again and the information reappears:

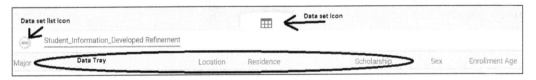

Using these features, you can add columns to the canvas by:

- Dragging them from the **Data Tray**.
- Selecting a column (or multiple columns) from the **Data set list**.
- Selecting a column from a *different dataset*. This is done by clicking on the **Data set list** icon and then clicking on the **<** icon to view and select a different dataset.

Besides adding columns of data, you can add *visualizations*, by clicking on the
Visualization icon (shown in the following screenshot) and selecting a visualization
type that you want to use:

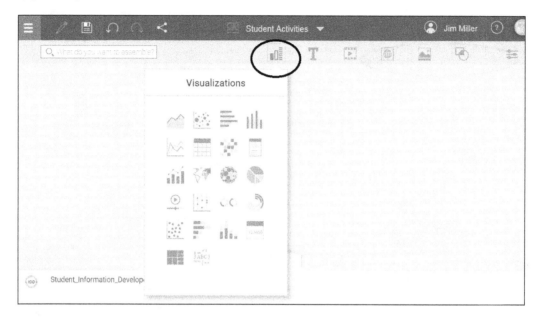

Moving to the right (from the **Visualizations** icon), we have additional icons that
provide various other options. These are, **Text**, **Media**, **Webpage**, **Image** and **Shapes**.
Each allows you to add and enhance your dashboard view.

The far-right icon (shown in the next screenshot) is the **Properties** icon. This icon
allows you to change your dashboard's *theme* and *general style*. At the time of writing
this book, only a few themes and styles are available, but more are planned:

Another option for enhancing your dashboard, should the aforementioned not be
sufficient, is to access your Watson Analytics collection by clicking on the collection
icon on the far right of the main toolbar shown in the following screenshot and
dragging selections from the collection list onto the dashboard canvas:

Finally, if nothing else suits your needs, you can have Watson Analytics create a new visualization based on a question you type in the **What do you want to assemble?** field, as follows:

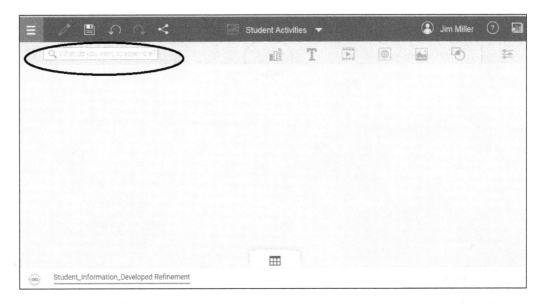

A simple use case

To gain a better understanding of how to use the Watson Analytics Predict and Assemble features, let's now take a look at a simple use case.

One of the best ways to learn a new tool is by using it, and to *use* Watson Analytics, you need data. Up to this point, we've utilized sample data for use cases that I created from various sources, but Watson Analytics has made many sample datasets available for use for your learning. To view the sample data options, simply click on **Add** from the main or **Welcome** page and then click on **Sample Data**, as shown in the following screenshot:

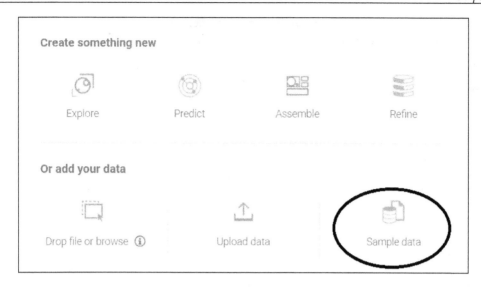

 For more information about the available Watson Analytics supplied sample data, you can go to https://community.watsonanalytics.com/resources.

For our use case, we'll go back to an example used earlier in this book—**Stadium Sales**. For this use case, we've received a similarly formatted file, but one that includes historical results of products sold by a particular NFL team at their home stadium over two previous seasons. The file, named Historic_Stadium_Sales, can be uploaded to Watson Analytics as explained in earlier chapters:

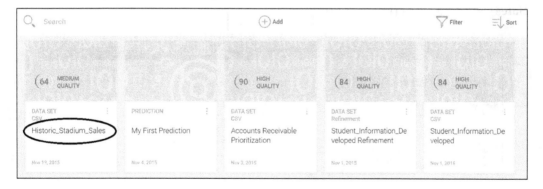

Once the file is uploaded (shown in the previous screenshot), you can click on the upper portion of the file's *tile* and then select **Predict**:

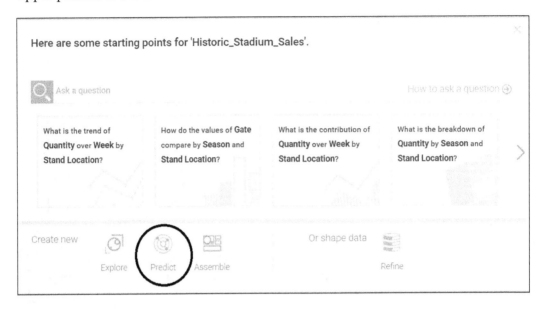

Remember, that you could've used the Watson Analytics **Refine** or **Explore** features on this file (as we have already covered), but since this file is really the same as the original stadium sales file, we feel that we are relatively comfortable with its format, so we'll just go ahead and try Watson Analytics' **Predict** feature.

After clicking on **Predict**, let's *name our workbook* (I've decided to call it **Historic Sales**) and *set a target* (I picked **Product**):

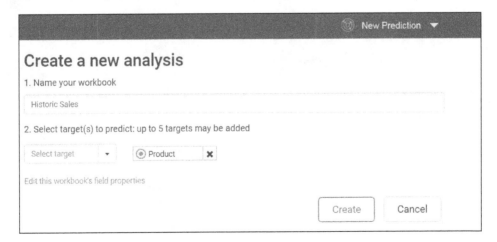

Next, click on **Create**. Watson Analytics, in *real time*, runs its *analytical algorithms* on our data and displays the following *insights*:

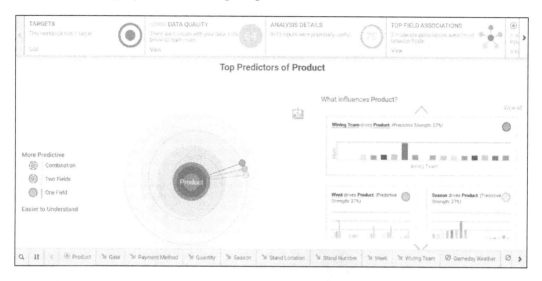

Watson Analytics has organized its results into various sections, so we can understand them more easily. Let's start from the center of the page, as shown in the following screenshot:

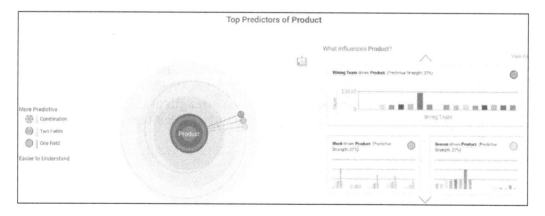

This section is focused on the *predictors of our selected target* (**Product**). In other words, which fields in our data have some *influence* on the value of **Product**? This is interesting, since I may be trying to determine which particular product sells best and when. Watson Analytics has found that three fields have some correlation to **Product**: **Winning team**, **Week**, and **Season**. I can easily set that by sliding my mouse arrow over the three *bullets* in the target:

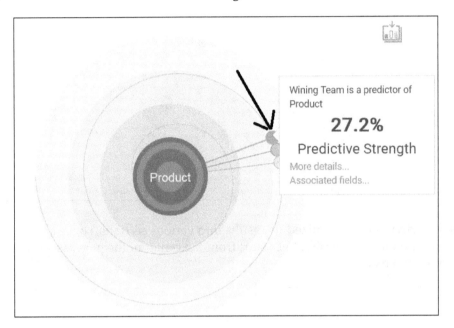

For example (as shown in the preceding screenshot), **Winning Team** is displayed as a *predictor bullet* of **Product** (as well as the other fields, **Week** and **Season**). From the bullet popup, you can see that **Predictive Strength** of **Winning Team** is *over 27 percent*, and you have the option to click on two links: **More details...** and **Associated fields....**

To the right of our *target*, the predictors are displayed in another way: **What influences Product?** Check out this screenshot:

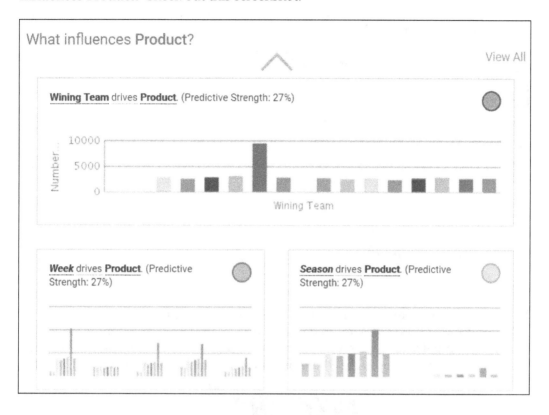

Since the *top predictor* (and the most intriguing one to me) is the **Winning team** field, let's look a bit closer at it. If you click on the **More details...** link from the bullet popup, or on the top visualization to the right of the target, Watson Analytics *zooms in to* the **Main Insight**:

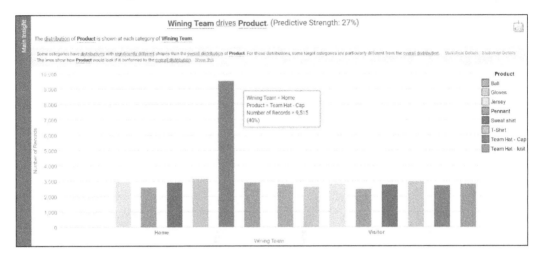

We can easily see from the visualization provided that when the home team wins, the most popular product seems to be **Team Hat - Cap**. This is easy for me to understand, but if you are interested in the statistical details of this insight, you can click on **Details** in the top-right corner of the visualization (shown here):

Since you are so inclined, Watson Analytics provides a brief explanation of how it arrived at the main insight (winning team drives product). Across the top of the details page, you see this statement:

Product is a categorical target, so a logistic regression based approach is used.

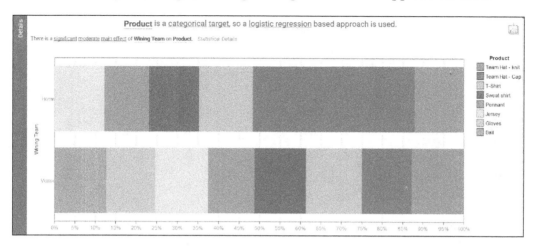

If you look closely, you'll notice that *categorical, target* and *logistic* regression are hyperlinks that will provide definitions and **Learn more** links if you click on them, as marked here:

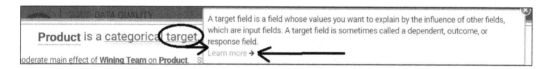

All throughout the prediction, look for the presence of these helpful hyperlinks to build your knowledge of the statistical theory behind Watson Analytics' insights. In addition, wherever possible, click on the **Collect** icon (shown in the following screenshot) to add to your collection of artifacts to be used later:

Back to the **Top Predictors** section, to the bottom left, we see **More Predictive** and **Easier to Understand**:

Watson Analytics starts with the easiest—**One Field** selected as a *start*. The **One Field** is **Winning Team**. You can experiment by switching to **Two Fields** (what two fields drive the product?) or **Combination** (is there a combination of fields that drive the product?) and see the results of your selection in real time.

Across the top of the prediction is the basic information band, as shown in this screenshot:

Here, Watson Analytics provides basic information, such as the following:

- **TARGETS**: This shows what the selected targets for this predictive analysis are (ours was **Product**)

- **DATA QUALITY**: This gives a rating of the predictive quality of the data, along with any issues or interesting facts

- **ANALYSIS DETAILS**: This indicates the number of potentially useful inputs for the analysis

- **TOP FIELD ASSOCIATIONS**: This shows the associations of certain fields within the data

- **TARGET MODEL INPUTS**: This is a *coming soon* feature of Watson Analytics

Across the bottom of the page is **Data Tray**; it lists all of the fields within our data file, as shown here:

From the **Data Tray**, you have the ability to drag fields into your prediction. For example, you can select **Quantity** and drop it onto the target to see that fields **Top Associations**. As shown in the following screenshot, Watson Analytics tells us that the **Winning Team** field is also associated with the value of **Quantity**; that is, when the home team wins, we have a higher number of products sold:

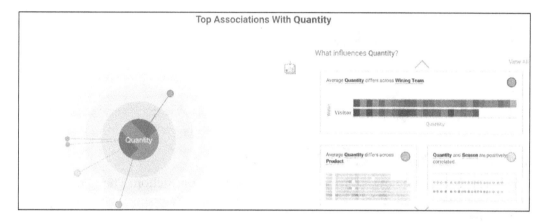

Finally, in the top-left corner is the **MENU** icon, from where you can access important Watson Analytics features, that is, **FIELD PROPERTIES** and **VERSIONS**:

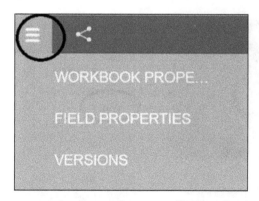

FIELD PROPERTIES lets you explore and change the statistical properties of each field in your data file. The fields are listed vertically on the left and the properties of the (selected) field are on the right. You can sort and filter the fields if you need to (if the number of fields is large, this is very helpful):

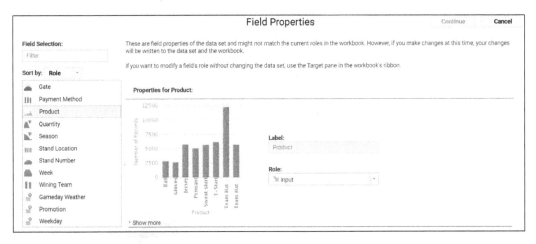

Some points of interest

Field roles determine how a particular field is used in a prediction. The role of a field can be changed by selecting the desired value from the **Role** drop-down list, as you can see here:

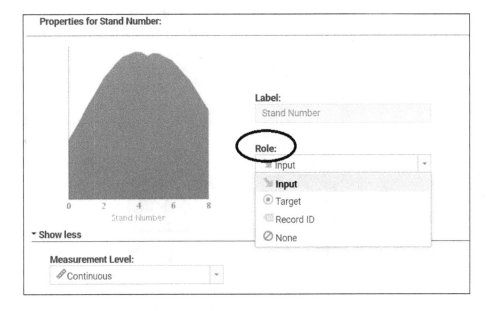

Measurement Level is used to classify a field for predictive analysis and can affect Watson Analytics' ability to identify insights. The measurement levels for a field can be changed by selecting them from the **Measurement Level** drop-down list, as shown in this image:

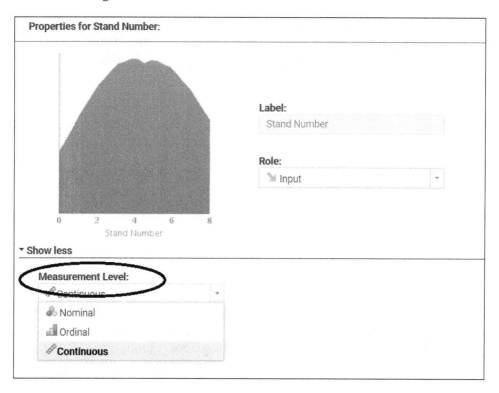

Data issues are also visualized here. In our example, the **Gameday Weather** field is supposed to hold the weather conditions on the day of the game. In our file, Watson Analytics has found that all records contain **Sunny**, which appears suspicious, so it excludes the field from further analysis:

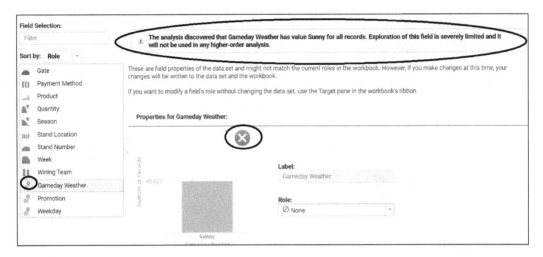

Versioning

When you change anything in the *field properties*, Watson Analytics automatically creates a *new version* of your prediction for you. Under **Menu** and then **Version**, you can view and access/reload any of those saved versions, as follows:

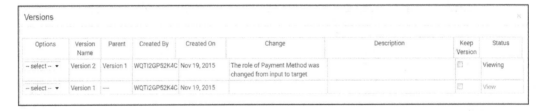

You should now understand **Predict**—at least enough to start experimenting with your data, so let's move on and take a look at **Assemble**.

Assemble

As we've mentioned earlier in this book, **Assemble** gives you the ability to present what you may have discovered using Watson Analytics in various ways, such as dashboards and stories. To illustrate, let's assemble a dashboard using our historical stadium sales prediction example that we just walked through.

From the Watson Analytics **Welcome** page, we click on **Add** and then on **Assemble**, like this:

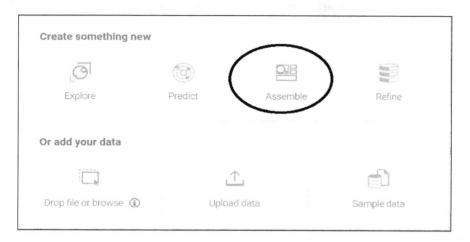

From the **Create new View** dialog, we select (double click on) our data, **Historic_Stadium_Sales**:

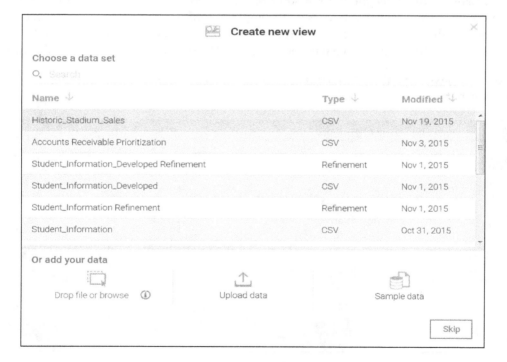

Watson Analytics will then display the **Create** page, like this:

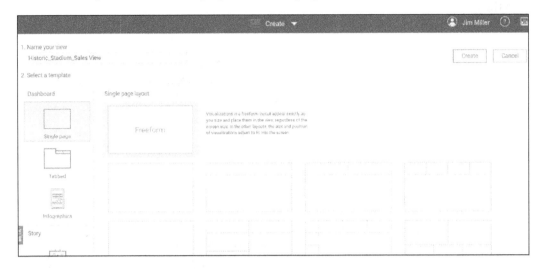

What I want to share with my colleagues is the results of our earlier prediction analysis—the main insight that Watson Analytics identified. That is, when the home team wins, team baseball cap sales go through the roof. To do that, I want to click on **Freeform** (shown in the preceding screenshot) and then on **Create** (in the top-right portion). For this example, we will stick to a simple single-panel, free-form dashboard.

Now we have a blank *canvas* to create our simple dashboard, as shown in this screenshot:

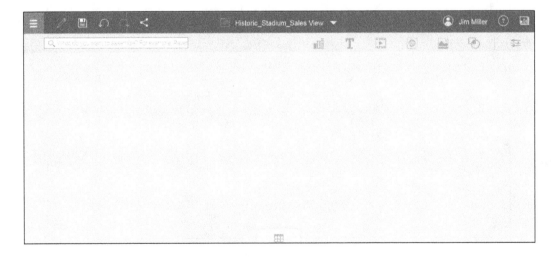

We'll perform three simple steps to assemble our dashboard.

First, let's add the **Historic Sales** visualization that we saved earlier by accessing the collection of artifacts. We do this by clicking on the collection icon in the top-right corner of the page, as shown in the following screenshot, and dragging the artifact onto our canvas:

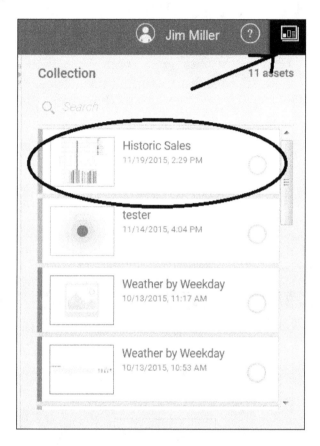

Once the visualization is on the canvas, you can resize it by adjusting its borders and sliding it to the exact position you want:

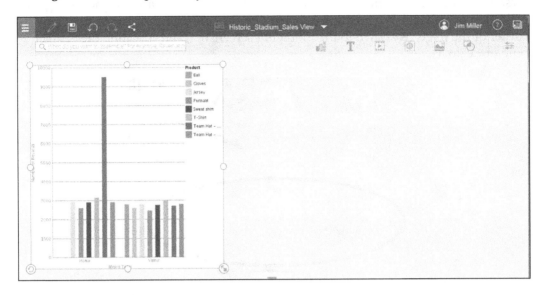

Next, let's add a bit of a banner to the dashboard by clicking on the **Text** icon and typing our message, as follows:

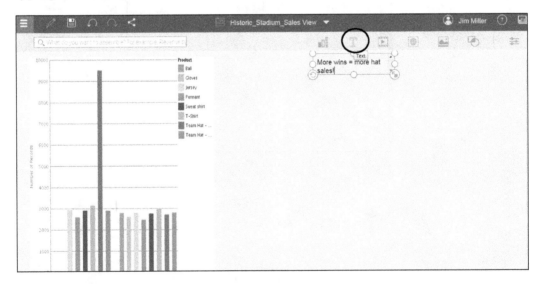

Then, let's include a photo of our latest team hat direct from our supplier, by clicking on the image icon and pasting a valid web address, like this:

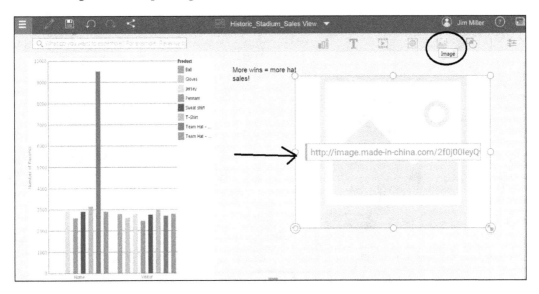

We can then resize and reposition our three artifacts the way we want them:

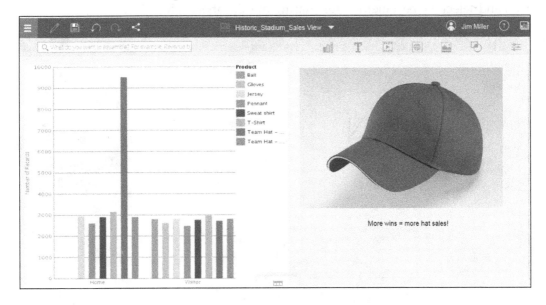

Finally, we can click on the **Save** icon and give our dashboard a name, as shown in this image:

Furthermore, this is too nice not to share with the team, so let's click on the share icon and select the best method for sharing our dashboard, like this:

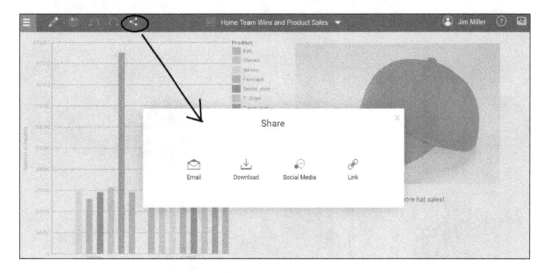

Summary

In this chapter, we went over Watson Analytics' Predict and Assemble, demonstrating how they work and how they can add value to insights identified with Watson Analytics Explore and Refine.

In the next chapter, we will discuss the idea of customizing and extending solutions created with IBM Watson Analytics.

6
Customizing and Extending

In this chapter, we will explore the concept of extending the power of Watson through the use of external tools such as IBM SPSS.

We've broken down the chapter into the following topics:

- What do we mean by extending?
- Using IBM SPSS
- An example use case

Meeting the requirements

Every tool or technology, no matter how powerful, cannot possibly meet every current as well as future requirement for all users. With this in mind, much of today's software provides options for developers to *customize* (to better fit a particular environment or user) and *add on or extend functionalities or features* (to best meet a particular use or need).

Customization and extension can range from simply configuring an online profile to programming with the provided **Application Programming Interfaces (APIs)**.

Reasons to customize or extend

Why would you be interested in customizing or extending a particular application or tool? There are a variety of reasons, but the simplest (which may apply best to Watson) are as follows:

- To adapt an interface—or access to—specific information or an application action (or actions) so that it is less generic and *more tailored* to a specific purpose
- To provide additional logic or processing that does not exist within the current application or tool

Customizing Watson

How can we customize our Watson experience? Well, Watson doesn't *really* offer customization as it is described in the previous section, but it does offer some opportunities to customize your experience. These include the following:

Subscriptions

The first, and maybe the least obvious, way of customizing Watson is through your *subscription*. We will go over upgrading your subscription in detail in the next chapter, but for now, it's worth mentioning that by simply upgrading from the free version, you can adjust the storage space, licenses, and subscription features that you have access to (all for an additional cost). This customizes Watson to, perhaps, provide more space or functionality that you need for your analysis.

Data

In Watson, you can customize the *appearance of data* in an exploration to better meet your requirements. You have the ability to change the *type or format* of a column of data (number, text, date, or time interval), *how the data is aggregated*, and the *names of columns*.

Changing column types

To change the type or format of a column of data in your file, you have to follow these steps:

1. *Select* the column in the Watson data tray that you want to reformat by clicking on it. Then click on the **Edit** icon, as shown here:

2. Click on the **Properties** icon:

    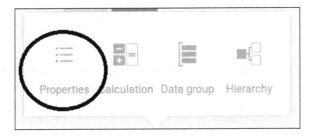

3. From the **Properties** popup, click on **Type**:

4. From the **Type** popup, click on the desired format for the column of data, as follows:

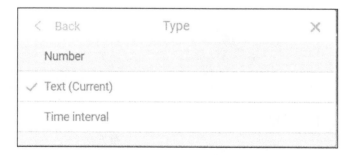

5. Close the **Properties** popup.

Custom reaggregation

Another way to customize *data* within Watson is by changing the *aggregation level* of your data. To accomplish this, you have to perform these steps:

1. *Select* the column in Watson **Data Tray** that you want to reaggregate by clicking on it. Then click on the **Edit** icon:

2. Click on the **Properties** icon:

3. Click on **Aggregation** and choose the desired method of aggregation:

4. Close the **Properties** box.

Customizing column names

Perhaps, the most common way of customizing data in Watson is by changing field or column names. To do this, you have to do the following steps:

1. *Select* the column in the Watson data tray that you want to rename by clicking on it. Then click on the **Edit** icon:

2. Click on the **Properties** icon:

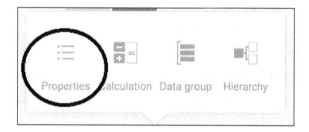

3. Next, click on **Change name**:

4. Type a new name for the column, and then close the **Properties** popup.

Persistence

Customizations should persist. Once you have taken time to set how you want your data to look, you should be done. Unfortunately, it doesn't work that way in Watson. If you want your changes to apply to all explorations, you have to make those very changes to each new data file that you upload.

Views

Another way you can customize your Watson experience is with views. You may recall from an earlier discussion that views are what *contains* Watson dashboards and stories, and you can *customize your views* in a variety of ways. Here is an example.

Once a view is created, you can customize the view by:

- Changing the view's *theme* or *presentation style*
- Changing its *properties*
- Changing the *media* (*web pages, images, shapes,* and so on) included in the view

In addition to this, you can add or duplicate tabs within your view, group or regroup objects, and even include data from other data files.

Changing themes and presentation styles

Every Watson theme has a predefined presentation style. You can easily change to a different theme, giving a view a totally new look and feel. To change the themes of an existing view, follow these steps:

1. Click on the **Edit** icon, as shown in the following screenshot, in the top-left corner of the icon bar:

2. Next, click on **Properties**:

3. Then click on **Themes**:

4. Finally, select the theme:

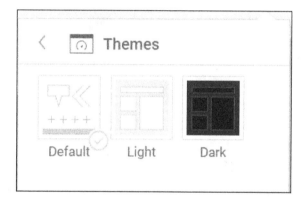

Changing properties

At the time of writing this book, Watson's view properties are pretty limited. These properties include view fill color, border color, and opacity:

1. To change a view property (assuming you are already in edit mode), click on **Properties**:

2. Then select **General style**:

3. Select your new background color from those shown:

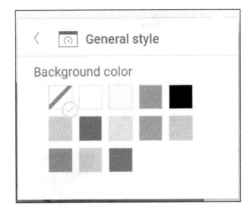

Changing the media

In an earlier chapter, we created a dashboard view and demonstrated how to add media such as a text banner, an image, or a web page (note that you can also embed a web page or other media, such as a video). You can use media to further customize your views by changing them to fit your needs, as follows:

1. Click on the **Edit** icon:

2. Then (to add new media) click on the **Media** icon that you want to add, as shown here:

3. To change the media that is already part of your view, click on the *media object* and then click on **Properties**:

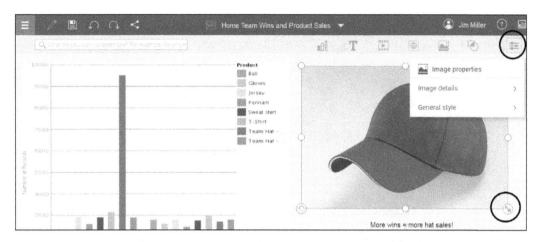

In the preceding screenshot, you can see that I have selected the image object (the red hat) and then clicked on **Properties**.

Tabs, grouping, and new data

If you have created your view with one or more tabs, you can further customize it by replicating a tab or tabs. You can do this by simply clicking on the *tab* that you want to replicate and then clicking on the **Duplicate** icon, as shown in the following screenshot:

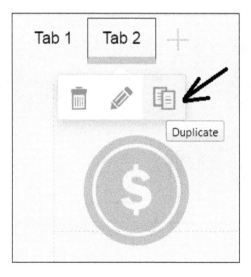

Grouping and regrouping of objects in a view is yet another way of customizing. You can simply click and hold two or more objects and then click on the **Group** icon (shown next):

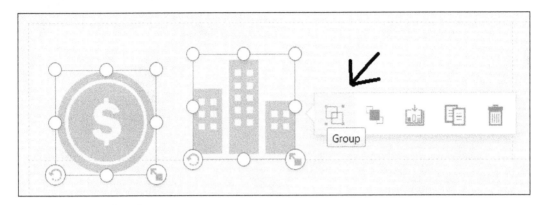

Finally, adding data to a view that exists in *other data files* is another of your view customization options.

To add data to your view from a different data file, *open the data tray* by clicking on the **Data Tray** icon at the bottom of the page, as shown in the following screenshot:

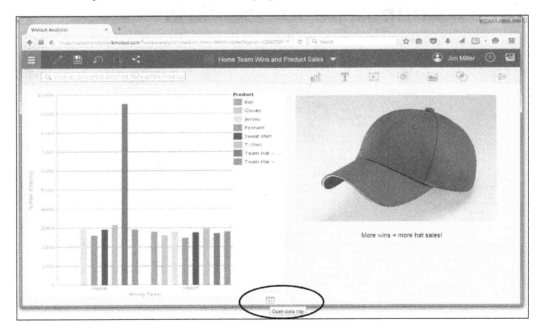

Next, in the left corner, click on the **Data set** icon:

The **Data set** icon will open the **Data sets list** popup (shown next). Here, you can scroll through and select one of the available (already uploaded to Watson) files:

Once you *select a data file* (by clicking on it), the fields in that file are listed and you can *scroll through* and *select* a field (again by clicking on it). Then, you can either *drag* the field onto your view or simply click on the **Add** button:

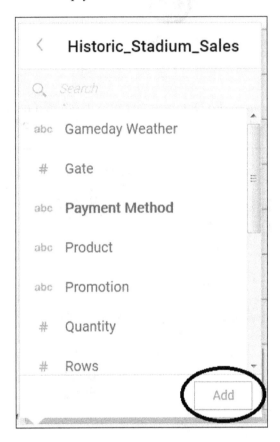

Extending Watson

We've already seen how IBM Watson can be used to *increase the value of* or *extend* the *results of your data analytics efforts* through easy exploration and visualization. This is accomplished with Watson's cutting-edge ability to understand your typed questions and provide unique, interactive visualizations that are based on your words. In the preceding section, we looked at ways by which you can customize your Watson experience. Now let's consider the prospects for *extending* Watson.

With all that Watson can do, it is still dependent on *data quality*. In other words, the better the data, the better the results.

Data quality

When you hear the term "data quality" in conjunction with Watson analytics, it refers to how *apt* certain data is for *performing analyses*. In other words, how reasonable might the results be if one performs an analysis with the data file?

In *Chapter 2, Identifying Use Cases*, we briefly mentioned that Watson assigns a *data quality score* to each dataset when you upload it. This score (from 0 to 100) is an assessment of the data's quality based on a *computed average* of the data quality *of each field or column* in the data file.

To compute the data quality score for a field in a data file, Watson considers the following factors:

- **Missing values**: Records or transactions that have *no data entered* in a particular field will affect the data's quality score. The more records with missing values, the lower the data quality score.

- **Constant values**: Some fields in your file may have the *same value for every field*, making the data quality score for these fields zero.

- **Imbalance**: An imbalance condition can occur if fields in a data file are defined as *categorical* and *records are not equally distributed across the defined categories* — this is known as *unequal frequency*. The more the unequal frequencies, the lower the data quality.

- **Influential categories**: Influential categories are categories that are significantly different from other categories and therefore have more influence over the field. As the influence of these categories increases, the data quality decreases.

- **Outliers**: Outliers are the *extreme values* found in a field (as compared to the average values of a field). The more the outliers, the lower the data quality.

- **Skewness**: Skewness measures *how symmetrically a continuous field is distributed*. Skewed fields have lower data quality scores.

Watson data metrics

In *Chapter 2, Identifying Use Cases*, we pointed out that Watson provides you with the ability to both *explore* and *refine* your data file. Recall that you can review and tune your data file to match the way you want to see or work with it, and any changes that you make are saved as a *separate version* of the original data file.

Let's look again at the `Historic_Stadium_Sales` file that we previously loaded into Watson:

Click on the file (as shown in the preceding screenshot) and then click on **Refine**, as shown here:

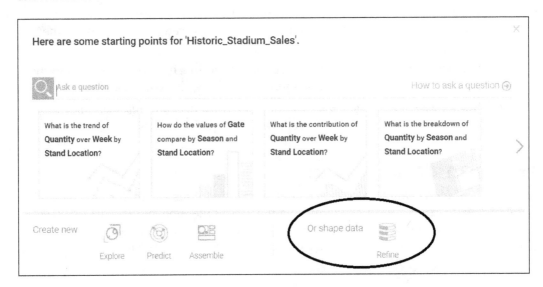

With our file displayed on the refine page (shown next), we have to click on the **Data Metrics** icon:

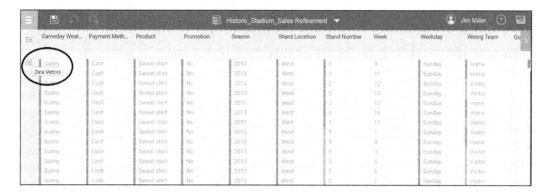

Watson then displays the data quality for each column of data:

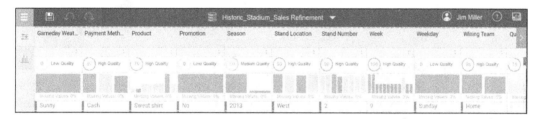

If you look closely at the **Gameday Weather** column, you'll see that the data quality score is *zero*:

This is because the value of the column of data is *constant* for all records (**Sunny** is the only value found). As we discussed earlier in this section, this affects the data quality of this column and ultimately the data quality of *the entire file*.

Here is another example of data quality. In the same file, Historic_Stadium_Sales, the column named **Payment Method** has a data quality score of **97**, as shown in this screenshot:

In a new version of this file that I uploaded, Historic_Stadium_Sales_ MissingValues, the same column has a much lower data quality score, which is **71**. If you look at the following score, you will see that Watson has found that **3%** of the records in this file have no value (they are missing) for the column:

Using IBM SPSS

The generally accepted process for preparing or *tuning* a data file for analysis in Watson is shown in the following figure:

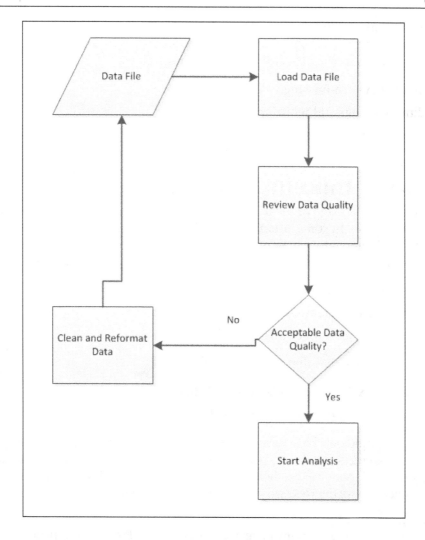

The process for preparing a data file in Watson is described in the following steps:

1. The data file is loaded into Watson.

2. You can use Watson to review the quality of the data in the file.

3. If the quality of the data is *unacceptable*, you can clean and/or reformat the data file and then reload the new version of the file into Watson.

4. If the quality of the data is *acceptable*, you can begin your analysis.

Steps 2 and 3 can be performed solely using Watson. However, you may want to consider *extending the process* by using a tool that may offer *specific data preparation* functionalities, such as the IBM SPSS modeler.

For example, earlier in this section, we saw that the **Payment Method** column contained *missing values* in **3%** of the records in the file. As it turns out, the IBM SPSS modeler is *built to recognize* several *types* of missing values:

- Null or system-missing values
- Empty strings and white space
- Blank or user-defined missing values

Handling missing values

Based on your knowledge of the data, you will be deciding to either *remove* the blanks or *fill them in*. In some situations, usually because of time, you'll just remove them. Those missing values may represent new business opportunities or additional insights. To choose the best approach, you should consider the following:

- How big is your data file?
- What is the total number of fields that contain blanks?
- What is the amount of missing information?

There are two approaches that you can take:

- You can exclude the fields or records that contain missing values
- You can impute, replace, or *coerce* the missing values

With IBM SPSS modeler, both approaches can pretty much be *automated* using what is called a *node*. Modeler nodes are classified as source, process, output, and modeling nodes depending on their function. Various nodes include the data audit node, the select node, the reclassify node, as well as source and output nodes.

 There are many more nodes provided in SPSS modeler; these are but a few.

With nodes, you can create *logic* that excludes records with fields that contain too many missing values, or assigns missing values for any or all of the fields. This is a powerful feature, allowing you to not only assess the quality of your data but also take action based on the assessment. In the next section, we will examine a sample use case that demonstrates the use of IBM SPSS modeler to extend Watson by automating the assessment and cleaning of a data file.

An example use case

As part of an effort to control underage students' drinking of alcoholic beverages at a university, the institution required each student to fill out an anonymous online survey on the topic. The students' demographical information was gathered (sex, age, major, credits completed, current GPA, and so on), as well as responses to questions such as *"Do you think it is okay to consume alcohol if you are underage"*, *"Have you ever consumed alcoholic beverages on campus"*, and so on. A file of the results of the survey was provided in comma-delimited format (CSV).

Following the procedure outlined previously (to tune data), the first step is to *load the file into Watson*.

As in our previous examples, from the **Welcome** page, click on **Add** and then on **Upload data**:

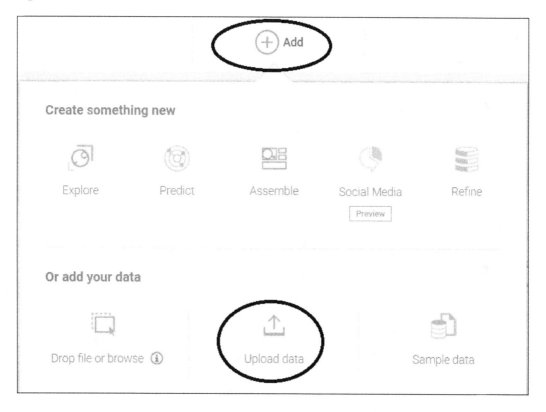

Then click on **Browse**:

The next step is *to review the data quality*. Once we have our file loaded into Watson, we can see that the overall data quality is *HIGH*, with a score of **77**:

Since the score shown is the *overall file* score, it is advisable to open the file in *refinement* mode and review the particular fields we are interested in.

Click on the file and then click on **Refine**:

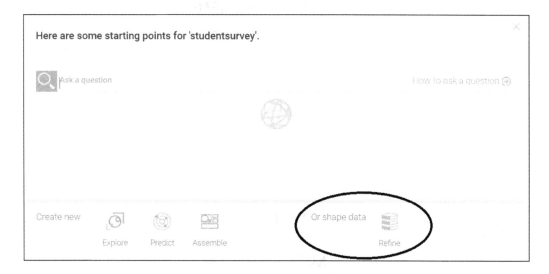

In **Refine**, you can see the columns (circled) that you are perhaps interested in. Even though the quality of the data is **High Quality**, you can see that some columns contain 22% missing values:

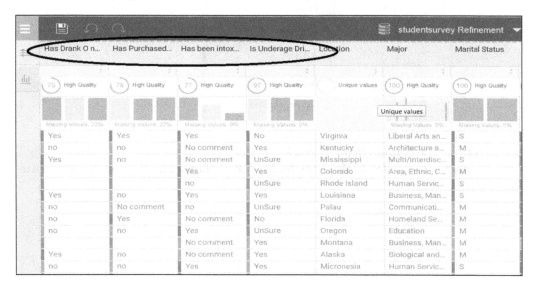

Additionally, if you scroll through the columns of data, you'll find that the **Sex** column has only *medium* data quality and a score of 67 (see the next image):

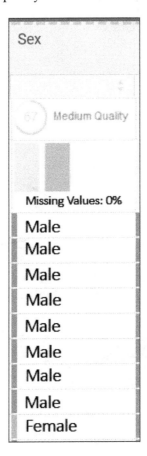

If you click on the column header, you'll discover that the column actually contains *five unique values*: **Male**, **Female**, **M**, **F** and **blank**. They are illustrated in the following screenshot:

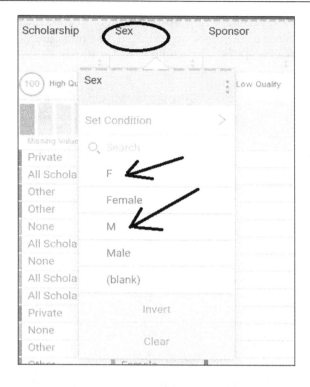

In this example, we will assume that *blanks* are *invalid responses*, and we should exclude all records from our analysis that contain blank as a value for the **Sex** field. Sometimes, you may want to further scrutinize blank values to determine whether a blank is a *non-response*, meaning it's a refusal to respond to a survey question. This may be a factor in predicting a specific outcome. Moving on, we will also assume that **M** means **Male** and **F** means **Female**, and the records should be considered valid and included as part of our analysis.

To *prove a point*, let's use IBM SPSS modeler to extend our Watson analysis by addressing the issues identified with the **Sex** field in our file.

 IBM SPSS modeler is an extremely powerful tool, and it is not the intention of the author to provide a complete tutorial or demonstration here. This is only to provide a simple example of how it can be used to automate data tuning and therefore *extend* IBM Watson.

To begin with, if we assume that we are going to periodically receive new student survey files (all in the same format), why not set up a process to run the file through that will evaluate identified issues with our data?

After opening modeler, I create a new stream, `WatsonStudentSurvey.str`. Next, to import our file, I include a `var` file source node. This node automatically reads data from delimited column text files, and all I'll do is browse to the filename and click on **OK**, as shown here:

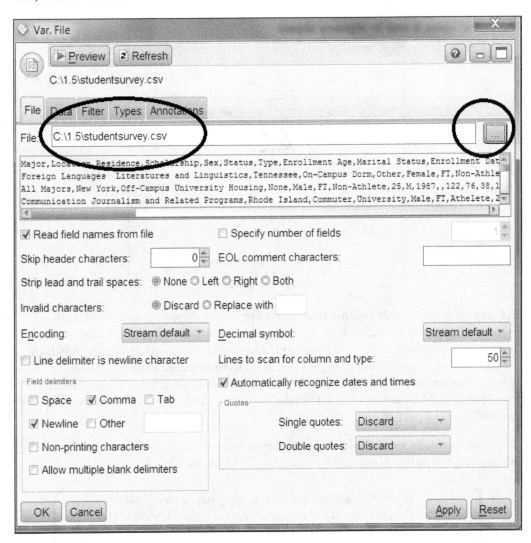

Next, I'll add the *record ops node* named **Select**. With this node, you can create a logical condition to include or exclude records. I'll use this node to drop all records in my file that have a blank value for the **Sex** column. On this node, I add the *logic condition* as **Sex=""**. Next, I click on **Discard** for the *mode*. Then I click on **OK**, as shown in the following image:

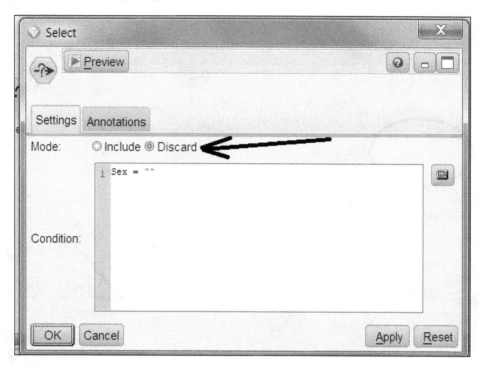

The *third node* to be used in our little example is the *field ops node*, **Reclassify**. This node will be used to *reclassify* the **M** and **F** values in the **Sex** field (as **Male** and **Female**, respectively). This requires only a few simple steps:

1. Select **Sex** under **Reclassify field**.
2. Indicate the original values, **M** and **F**.
3. Indicate the new values, **Male** and **Female**.
4. Click on **OK**.

Shown in the following screenshot:

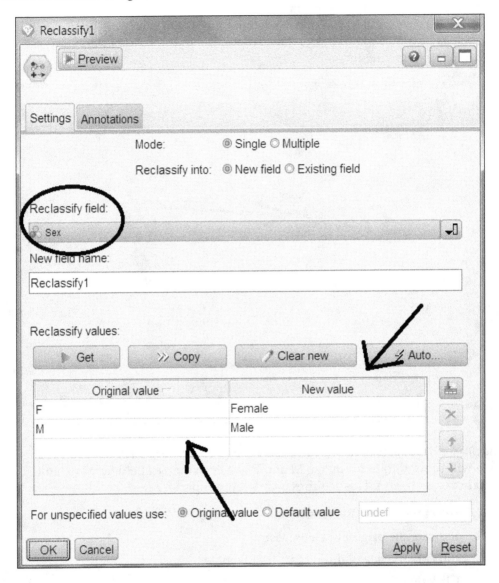

The final node will be *export node* **Flat File**. This node will be used to export our updated file back to a CSV to be imported to Watson. For this node, I can indicate the name and location for modeler to write to and then click on **OK**:

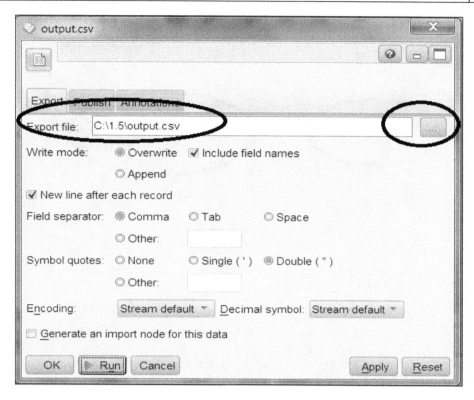

The connected nodes in our data tuning stream are as follows:

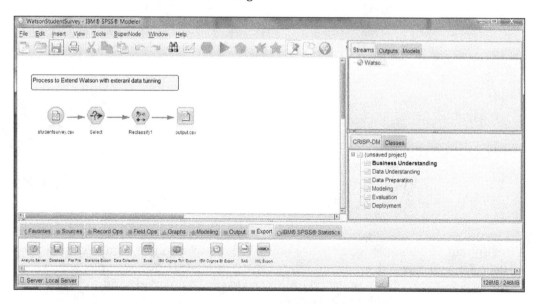

After uploading our *tuned* file, we see that the new file has a better overall file data quality score:

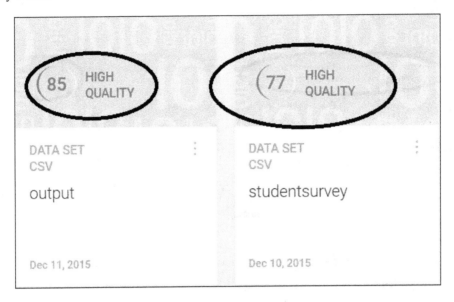

In refine page, we can locate our new column (the modified **Sex** column named **Reclassify1**) and see that its data quality score is **100**:

With this simple example, you can see how SPSS modeler can be used to extend Watson with an external, automated data tuning process. In our example, we addressed a single column of data, but this can easily be adapted to address just about any issue in any column of your file.

Back in Watson, running a prediction on our file produces (perhaps) a few interesting insights:

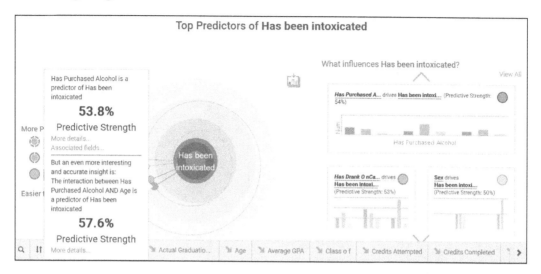

Summary

In this chapter, we went through the concept of customizing and extending an existing application or tool, what it means, and why you would be interested in it. In addition, we discussed what these terms mean to Watson—and how it can be customized and extended—to better fit your specific requirements. IBM SPSS modeler was introduced as a way of extending Watson to preprocess data, and finally a use case was covered to better illustrate the idea of extending a Watson Analytics analysis effort.

In the next chapter, we will prepare you to think more from an *enterprise perspective* when using IBM Watson.

7
Taking It to the Enterprise

In this chapter, we will prepare you to think from an *enterprise* perspective when using IBM Watson. We've broken down the chapter into the following topics:

- Understanding the *enterprise perspective*
- An enterprise Watson roadmap
- Upgrading your Watson edition
- Next steps
- An enterprise use case

Introducing an enterprise perspective

In this book, we started out by providing a definition of Watson and then walked you through accessing the tool for the very first time. In addition, we covered the Content Analytics architecture; discussed what a *classic* analytics cycle involves; explained the term use case; covered detailed building collections using Watson to *Explore*, *Predict*, and *Assemble* insights; and saw how you can *customize* and *extend* your Watson experience.

At this point, you should be somewhat comfortable with what might be referred to as *tactical Watson use* and are now ready to consider Watson from a *strategic* or *enterprise* perspective. When we say strategic, we mean doing things in a proven way and, specifically, looking for opportunities to gain an edge through the development and management of (Watson use) knowledge (and knowledge objects of your Watson collection).

Definition of Watson knowledge

Watson (from a strategic perspective) starts with your understanding that as you use and develop the Watson technology within your organization. The knowledge and experience you and your coworkers acquire and/or advance are characterized as your *knowledge of Watson* or *knowledge objects* (artifacts or assets created and saved to a Watson collection).

This *knowledge* can typically be organized into one of five different categories:

- Data interpretation
- Classification or grouping of data
- Data enrichment
- Normalization and modeling
- Collections

Let's see more about these in the next subsections.

Data interpretation

The process of understanding the data files you upload to Watson begins with the identification and extraction of certain *data points* or *fields* (from a raw data file or data source). Using the Watson Explore feature (or an external tool), you can learn to focus on specific (or default) fields that will help bring explicit meaning to the data, which otherwise might not always be evident. Additional fields may also be (manually) added to your data to expand upon and improve the organizations level of understanding.

Classification or grouping of data

You can decide to classify or *group together* data into *interesting sets of corresponding data events* before uploading it to Watson. These *combined files* are those that your organization has discovered through prior explorations or internal knowledge of the data source.

Data enrichment

Again, your data files can be *enriched* through the use of the Watson Explore feature or an external tool using *renaming*, *aggregation*, *computations* (in the form of formula fields) and so on. This can easily extend the helpfulness of data in numerous ways.

Normalization and modeling

You can use external tools to *normalize and model* your organizations collections of field information, group your sets of associated field values, and add *extracted fields* (from other data sources). You can *tag* different fields in your data as *the same* or perhaps give different fields aliases to make Watson *treat them the same*.

Collections

Over time, as you work with Watson, you can begin *collecting* your work created during Explore, Predict, and Assemble. In Assemble, you can also save other artifacts, such as images. Artifacts in your collection can then be reused in dashboards and stories that you create later.

Watson object management

Whether you are your organizations *sole Watson user* or one of a larger number of individuals using Watson within a team, sooner or later you will be faced with an ever-growing list of artifacts in your collection (perhaps referred to as Watson knowledge objects). In the most vivid example, organizations that have multiple individuals using Watson may even have a number of duplicate objects saved.

You may at some point find yourself:

- Sorting through a large Watson collection
- Interpreting misleading or conflicting names given to objects saved within a collection (more on this later in this chapter)
- Struggling to just find existing objects
- Recreating objects that have already been created or even shared

To that end, even a *minimalist effort* to organize and manage your organization's (or your own) collections can provide practical returns.

Organizational efforts include:

- **Simple inventory and organization**: Time should be taken to inventory and monitor your Watson collection to minimize the *reinvention* of objects that *solve* the same thing and promote useful *general purpose* objects that are created and shared on a global basis, across deployments.

- **Standardized normalization and modeling of data**: As mentioned earlier in this chapter, data files can (and most likely should) be explored and enriched by various means — internally (in Watson), or using an external tool or technology.

- **Standardizing on Version**: Organizations serious about using Watson should demand that all Watson users be on the same version — optimally the Professional version (more on this later in this chapter). In addition, *within* Watson, there is a provided *versioning feature* for your predictions (more on this later in this chapter as well).

Naming for documentation

As with any technology, it is *highly recommended* that you develop naming conventions (sometimes referred to as a naming *style*) for your knowledge objects (including the files you upload to Watson, and any data sources you set up using the professional version of Watson) *before* you begin developing them or using them. *That* is the trick.

Developing the naming conventions

It is difficult to create workable conventions or standards unless you have experience and are familiar with what objects can be created within Watson and each objects purpose. Generally speaking, more mature organizations will adopt styles used with other technologies, which you'll need to learn and adhere to. In new or less mature shops, it'll be up to you.

You can cultivate naming conventions for almost every kind of knowledge object in Watson, but what will this standard naming really do for you?

Organized naming conventions

Using *consistent naming*, for example, a prefix for all objects intended for a specific purpose, will naturally show *object associations*. If I prefixed all of the objects created for demoing in this book with **book_demo_**, then they would easily stand out (from all the other objects in my Watson collection). Additionally, I could be more specific, like naming all of the dashboards **book_demo_dashboards_**. This would create groups within my *book demo* list of objects.

Object naming conventions

Object naming can also be used to *describe the purpose* of an object. For example, an object named `historic_stadium_sales_` indicates that the object focuses on the historic stadium sales file. You might want to include the following information in the object name:

- The type of object (dashboard, prediction, company logo image, and so on)
- The file name used (for a Watson Prediction, for example)
- The timeframe represented
- Its purpose

Hints

- **Start early**: The sooner you start adopting a convention or style the better, since later (once there are potentially many, many objects already created and in use) it will be confusing to have to *sift through* and rename, and so on.

- **Be consistent**: Make sure that you choose a style that can be easily followed by you and all of the users in your organization. If everyone *consistently* follows the convention, it will become easier to use as time goes by.

- **Be reasonable**: Use a style/convention that makes sense and is easy to understand and use. If you don't, the convention will most likely be abandoned or at least avoided. In addition, use conventions only when *it makes sense* to do so, not *just because* it is the standard.

- **Forward think**: At this time, I do not believe that there is any *globally adopted* Watson standard naming convention or style, but it does make sense to adopt one of your own and offer it to the Watson online community. This way, you may receive constructive feedback and perhaps play a role in standardizing the technology!

Testing

Everyone involved with the development or delivery of software or technology solutions is aware of the importance of testing. Testing (or at least *validating*) what you create using Watson will allow for stakeholders to appreciate and comprehend the insights identified and shared with less concern for the correctness of the base information that the insights may be based upon.

Testing is a huge subject and beyond the scope of this book, so I will simply state the obvious: *insights, no matter how exciting, are dangerous if based upon incorrect or invalid data or data taken out of context*. Therefore, it is strongly advised to validate your data *before* making decisions based upon Watson outcomes.

There are an endless number of approaches to solution testing but with Watson solutions, you'll benefit most from *preparation* and *preprocessing*. In *Chapter 2, Identifying Use Cases*, we went over the importance of properly defining a use case, what to ask your data and putting your data into proper context. This is what we call **preparation**. In *Chapter 3, Designing Solutions with Watson Analytics* we covered data considerations and how to use the Watson *Explore* functionalities to handle data considerations or **preprocess** your data (we also touched on extending Watson in *Chapter 6, Customizing and Extending* by using external tools to explore and preprocess your data).

Test before sharing

If you intend to *share* your Watson insights you might want to establish *approval criteria* to determine whether your *share* is ready for *other eyes*. These criteria might include the following:

- Has the *data been validated* based upon any particular standards?
- Is the data in an *appropriate context*?
- *What use case* are we solving for?
- Is this considered intellectual property? Does it involve any existing IP? Is it *confidential in anyway*?
- Are the insights generally *sensible* or *reasonable*?
- Did you follow any formal data or object version control?

The enterprise vision

The *enterprise* or *strategic* vision for Watson (as with most tools and technologies) is based upon an *evolutionary roadmap* that begins with the initial evaluation of and experimenting with (Watson), to the *predicting and assembling* and finally (hopefully) the management and optimization of your organization's Watson use.

Evaluation and experimentation

This initial phase will generally cover the discovery and evaluation that takes place with any new (to the organization) tool or technology. Testing should cover everything required to determine if the tool/technology will meet or exceed the organizations needs now and into the foreseeable future. Once a decision is made to move forward, this phase also includes the installation, configuration, and everything that may be involved in deploying the new tool or technology for use by the intended users of the organization.

From a Watson perspective, this phase may involve accessing the *free version*, before upgrading and subscribing to a premium version of Watson. In addition, Watson should be validated using actual data samplings, in an environment comparable to the environment that will eventually be used. The Watson documentation advises that output from Watson may differ somewhat when using certain operating systems: *the results obtained in other operating environments may vary significantly*.

Predicting and assembling

Once you've accessed Watson for the first time, you'll begin exploring, predicting, and assembling. The effectiveness at which these events occur and the level of quality of those developed artifacts or *assets* (more on this topic later in this chapter) will be contingent upon the (hopefully escalating) level of experience (of Watson) that you possess. Characteristically, the exploration and use of Watson will be recurrent with each success.

Watson is a commanding instrument and, in *most cases*, does not necessitate extensive training to begin using. With human nature being what it is, once a reasonable output is realized and is validated as correct and valuable, it will be set aside for later reuse and, hopefully, pooled as a valuable *knowledge object* across the group or entire organization (either through a manual share or, if you have upgraded your Watson to a premium version, you can share collections more easily).

Although most organizations do eventually reach this phase, it is not unusual to see:

- Objects (everything from duplicated files, predictions, dashboards and stories) with similar or duplicate functionality
- Poor naming of objects (you've forgotten the details of the artifact so simply recreated what you need now)
- Objects not shared (but kept in collections indefinitely)
- Objects that are obsolete or do not yield expected results

Management and optimization

At some point, usually while (or after a certain amount of) artifacts are developed, the *process will mature*. Process maturity starts with beginning to devote time and perhaps dedicating resources to organize, manage and optimize what has been developed and saved (or in other words, perform *organizational knowledge management*).

You should consider forming a *governing committee* to support the identification and management of your Watson knowledge within your organization to:

- Record and appraise Watson output and insights
- Establish suitable naming standards and styles
- Establish suitable process and development standards
- Create, implement, and impose a strict validation strategy
- Continually develop *a vision* for Watson within your organization and the worldwide Watson community

More on the vision

As I've mentioned before, as a part of taking a strategic or enterprise approach to Watson, you'll need to develop a *vision*. This will ensure that your organization is able to leverage Watson to achieve the highest rate of return today and over time. This is not simply uploading data files and creating predictions, but it involves everything (and more) that we've discussed in this chapter best practices and *continued improvement of Watson skills.*

Enterprise Watson roadmap

Our enterprise Watson roadmap starts with a transitory account of IBM Watson. It is reported that research began on Watson in early 2006. Watson made its first public appearance with the *Jeopardy challenge* in February of 2011. It was *brought to market* with a focus on healthcare in August of that same year. In March of 2012, Watson expanded its focus to financial services and then added cross-industry solutions later that year.

So, what's next? It's very hard to tell. It has been said that Watson will *transform research, analytics,* and *human-machine interaction* and its creators have certainly invested in that promise. In my opinion, it's up to you to experiment and evaluate Watson for yourself and then decide.

Upgrading Watson

Part of your enterprise roadmap must eventually include upgrading to (ultimately) the professional version of IBM Watson. Simply put, you start with the *free version* for your *test drive*, upgrade to the *personal version* to develop your *personal* expertise, and you *go pro* (with the *professional version*) when you are ready.

Let's *revisit* the differences between the currently available versions of IBM Watson.

The free version

What do you *get for nothing?* In this case, *a lot.* The free version gives you all of Watson's core functionalities (access to cognitive, predictive and visual analytics) and lets you experiment and evaluate on your own schedule. Keep in mind that once you register as a Watson user you also have access to the Watson online communities.

The free version includes:

- Web access for 1 user
- Limit of 100,000 rows and 50 columns (per data file)
- 500 MB of storage
- Ability to upload delimited files and Microsoft Excel files

The personal version

In the personal version of Watson, you get all of the free version features, access to Twitter data, and the ability to work with larger data files:

- Web access for 1 user
- 1,000,000 rows and 256 columns limit (per data file)
- 2 GB of storage
- Ability to upload delimited files and Microsoft Excel files
- Access to more sources of data
- Access to social data from Twitter

Professional

When your organization is ready, the Watson professional edition adds support for a *multi-user environment* for collaboration and more data connectors. Note that even the product documentation is version specific, that is, information documenting these features is only available after you upgrade: *You need a Watson Analytics Professional edition account to get access to the database connections*:

- Allows multiple web users
- 10,000,000 rows and 500 column limit (per data file)
- 100 GB of storage
- The ability to upload delimited files and Microsoft Excel files
- Access to more sources of data, including IBM DB2, dashDB, SQLDB, Microsoft SQL Server, MySQL, Oracle and PostgreSQL (as of this writing)
- Access to social data from Twitter
- Ability to connect to IBM Cognos report data
- Access to share data sets, refined data sets, explorations, predictions, and views

Next steps

It is my opinion that the free version (the *Freemium* version) offers every feature you'll need to *evaluate* Watson. Frankly, the personal edition doesn't add enough (per file limits can be overcome programmatically externally to Watson and with some simple *space used* administration) so I'd recommend that when you are ready to upgrade, you go for the professional version. What really adds value is the additional data source support, the *multiuser environment*, and the ability to share (data sets, refined data sets, explorations, predictions, and views). In the next chapter, we will walk through the upgrade process (from the free version to the professional version) and explore some of the features found only in that (the professional) version.

An enterprise use case

Again for illustration, let's consider a sample use case and use some of the *enterprise oriented concepts* we discussed in this chapter.

This sample use case involves an organization that provides state-wide transportation for hire services. The group started with a couple of drivers, a car, and a van and has evolved into a large team of professional drivers offering (driving) services for individuals and specific events using a vehicle chosen from a fleet of specialized vehicles. At the request of management, all *trip information* is captured and saved by each driver and submitted to the main office at the end of each month as a part of the payment and expense reimbursement process. The objective is to perhaps gain some insights, such as:

- When are trip issues or unplanned events most likely to occur? For example do they most often happen on overnight trips?

- What can we expect for a tip (gratuity) based upon the run or event? For example, do corporate events or trips with multiple destinations tip better?

- Is there a relationship between the event type and vehicle type used? For example, do certain events require a certain type of vehicle?

The following information is requested in each file:

- **Run Date**: The date the trip began/started.

- **Pickup/Drop Locations**: Where the customer was picked up and dropped off (drop-off could be different from the pickup location).

- **Primary and Secondary destinations**: What was the planned destination(s)?

- **Vehicle Type**: The type of vehicle used for the trip.

- **Event Type**: For example, was this an athletic event, a wedding, or a corporate event?

- **Trip Type**: Whether or not the trip was an *overnight* (did the driver and vehicle not return the same day)

- **Tip grade**: This is not an amount. It is simply an indication of whether the customer tipped the driver consistent with the cost and effort of the service and vehicle involved.

- **Customer Type**: Was this a new customer, referral, or existing?

- **Guide**: Was a tour guide included in the trip?

- **Issues**: Did any unplanned events occur on the trip (an accident or illness)?

- **Type of payment rendered**: Was payment paid through an invoice, check or credit card?

Before *jumping into* Watson with our data files, let's take a moment to contemplate a few *points of interest* from an enterprise perspective:

- Since we are collecting and merging data from various sources (the organizations many drivers), we can expect that we may receive files in (slightly?) different formats. We will need to reformat them into a common format for Watson to process and, since we want to do this on an ongoing basis, we may continue to receive files that we'll have to again, reformat.

- In addition, management has requested that trip information be captured in MS Excel worksheets and sent by the first of the following month, but no other requirements were given to the drivers, therefore, inconsistencies in actual data *values* are present, requiring *interpretation*. For example, the field **Tip Grade** uses both scales **Large**, **Medium**, **Small**, and **None**, as well as a numbered scale of **3**, **2**, 1, and **0**. Blanks are also used to mean *no tip given* or *none*. Another example is the field **Overnight**, where we expect the value to be **Yes** or **No**, but it seems some drivers have provided a numeric value: **0** meaning not an overnight trip, or a number greater than zero to indicate the number of nights the trip actually took.

- Finally, since any insights garnered from the process of collecting and formatting the files each month needs to be presented to management in a *consistent manner*, and since (most likely) this process will be performed by different individuals each time, it would be helpful to establish some method of easily identifying artifacts validated and used in prior months.

Enterprising suggestions

As we have demonstrated in *Chapter 6, Customizing and Extending*, this modeler is a very viable option for extending your Watson analytical experience. It even offers you the ability to save and reuse what you create. Reformatting fields, interpreting field values, and merging or appending files are all *easily accomplished* with this tool.

Furthermore, as we have demonstrated throughout this book, Watson itself supports the saving of artifacts (visualizations, for example) in a collection for later reuse.

Let's now look at our sample use case, using the previously mentioned enterprise oriented suggestions.

Gather the files

Once the drivers have submitted their files, we can save them all in a single, secure location and verify that they are named in a consistent manner. We've used the prefix `BusRuns_` and a driver denotation of `_driver_nnn`:

`BusRuns_driver_001.csv`, `BusRuns_driver_002.csv`, `BusRuns_driver_003.csv`

Modeler streaming

Once the files are gathered, we can use IBM modeler to set up and save a *stream*. Again, this book is not intending to instruct on modeler, but a *stream* is the main *document type* used by IBM modeler. Your streams can be saved, re-loaded, re-edited, and re-executed. Streams can also be set up to run from a script and take parameters, global values, execute other scripts, and so on.

Our simple stream can:

- Read the individual driver files, rename columns, and interpret specific data values. The same logic can be applied to all of the driver files, or each file can have its own unique logic.

- Merge/append all of the individual files into a single file (remember, if you are not on the professional version, you may run into row/record limitations).

- Write out a single, consistently named file (ready for uploading to IBM Watson).

The following screenshot shows our simple SPSS modeler stream:

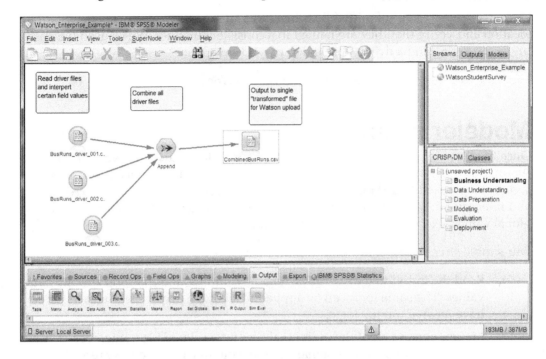

Upload to Watson

Once our process has created our combined file, we can upload it to Watson. The steps are as follows:

1. From the **Welcome** page, click on the plus icon and then click on **Browse** (shown in the following screenshot):

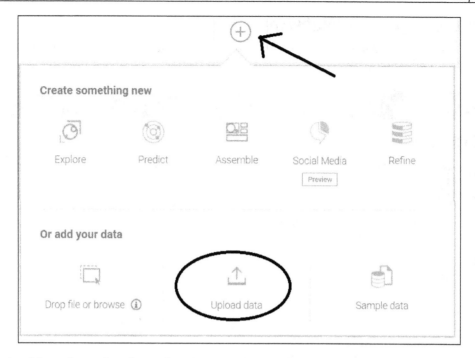

2. Next, (as we've done elsewhere in this book), browse to your file, select it, click on **Open**, and wait for the file to appear:

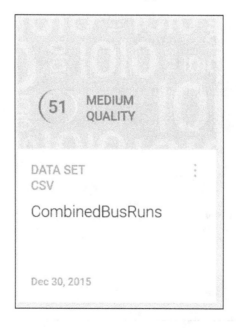

Predicting with Watson

Once our file is available to Watson, we can start with our analysis. We can start with a **Predict**. Let's start with a single **Target** of **Trip Issues**:

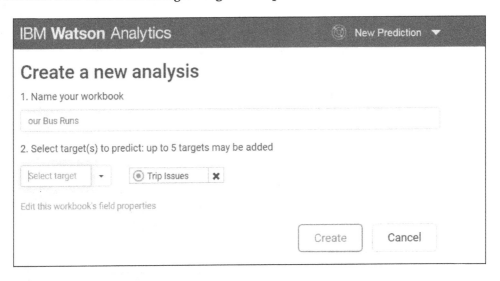

Watson provides our **Top Predictors** for our **Target (Trip Issues)**, which is shown in the next screenshot. Notice the **Collect** icon on the upper-left corner:

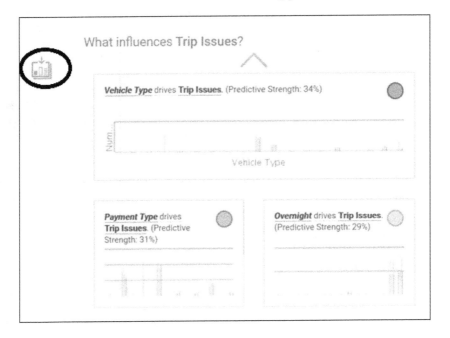

Clicking on the **Collect** icon adds to our collection. This is not really what you would expect though; **our Bus Runs** has been added to the collection (see the following screenshot), but it's not very helpful for later use because the name is so vague:

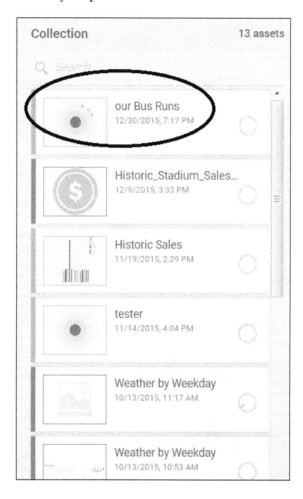

From an enterprise naming perspective, you should strive to be *very specific* with your predict name. Once it's created, it is somewhat difficult to rename. For example, going back to the main **Welcome** page and clicking on the **Predict** panel, you can click **Rename**:

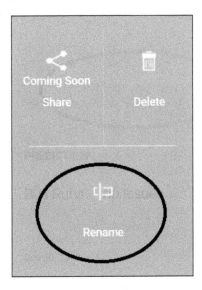

Then, you can give it a more descriptive name, like **Bus Runs – Trip Issues**.

But, be aware that if you open that prediction and click on the **Collect** icon, Watson still saves the **Predict** under the original name:

Our collected artifacts can be seen on the screen:

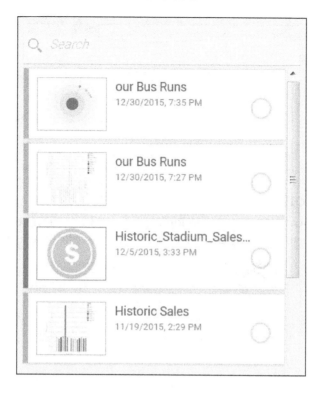

The only way to properly name our artifact is to *create a new Prediction* (with the same file and target) and name it what we want:

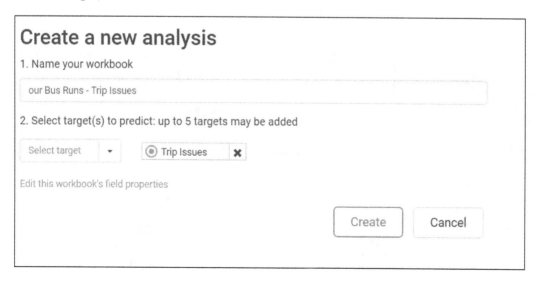

Then, add this prediction to our collection (using the **Collect** icon):

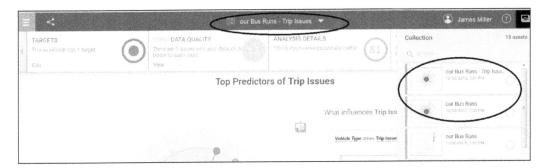

Watson versions

To demonstrate how Watson uses versioning, let's edit our prediction, changing our **Target** from **Trip Issues** to **Tip Grade** (as shown in the following screenshot):

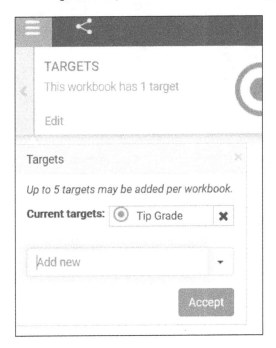

Next, using the **Versions** feature of Watson, click on the **Properties** icon (shown in the following screenshot) in the upper-left corner:

Then, select **VERSIONS**:

The **Versions** feature of IBM Watson *does* supply *some* help by adding a *Change Description*:

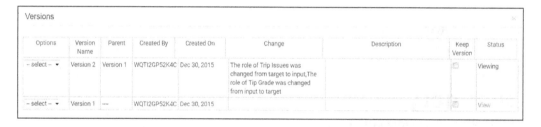

Options	Version Name	Parent	Created By	Created On	Change	Description	Keep Version	Status
– select – ▾	Version 2	Version 1	WQTI2GP52K4C	Dec 30, 2015	The role of Trip Issues was changed from target to input, The role of Tip Grade was changed from input to target		☐	Viewing
– select – ▾	Version 1	---	WQTI2GP52K4C	Dec 30, 2015			☐	View

This *new version* still *Collects* using the *same predict name:*

You can see that, without taking care to use proper naming conventions, versions and collections can quickly become `more of a burden than a useful resource.

Summary

In this chapter, we introduced the concept of an enterprise perspective when using Watson, looked at a simple roadmap for Watson (past, present, and future), discussed upgrading your version of IBM Watson, provided *next steps*, and then finished with another sample use case that illustrated some enterprise perspective use of Watson.

In the next chapter, we will look at the professional version of Watson and how Watson can add value to IBM Cognos Business Intelligence, a web-based, integrated business intelligence suite by IBM that provides a toolset for reporting, analysis, score carding, and monitoring of events and metrics.

8
Adding Value with Integration

In this chapter, we will discuss the importance of *integrating* Watson with various data sources, including IBM Cognos Business Intelligence (BI) reporting, and provide the steps required to perform such integrations. Finally, we will offer additional resources for you to continue your study of IBM Watson.

The chapter is organized as follows:

- Upgrading to Watson Professional
- Adding data source connections
- IBM Cognos BI
- Integration steps
- More learning opportunities
- Available references and material
- Getting help

Upgrading to Watson Professional

As we've mentioned in *Chapter 7, Taking It to the Enterprise*:

"Part of your enterprise roadmap must eventually include upgrading to (ultimately) the professional version of IBM Watson. Simply put, you start with the free version for your *test drive*, upgrade to the personal version to develop your *personal* expertise, and when you are ready, you *go pro* (with the professional version)."

To that end, let's now go over the process of upgrading to Watson Professional. Once you have logged in to Watson, you can click on your name and select either **My account** or **Upgrade**, as shown here:

I recommend that you click on **My account**. If you click on **My account**, you have the opportunity to review the space you are currently consuming and your data limitations and, if you have one, enter a promotion code (promotion codes are codes provided by IBM or their partners for limited free or discounted use of Watson). If you are working for an IBM partner, your employer may be able to provide you with such a promotion code:

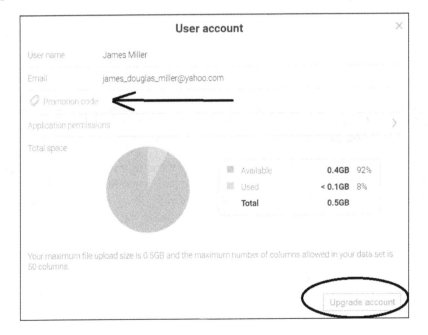

Once you click on the **Upgrade account** button (circled in the preceding screenshot), you enter **Cloud Shop**, where you can click on **Purchase** as shown in the following screenshot:

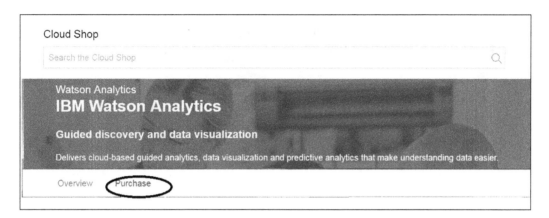

From there you can *scroll down* to where you see the **Professional** edition selection shown, and click on **Configure and buy**:

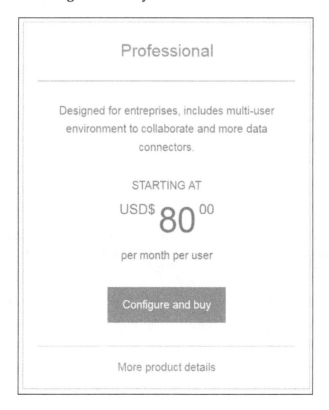

Once you click on **Configure and buy**, you have the option to change the number of users authorized to use your subscription to Watson, as well as add more disk space, before you continue to the checkout.

 Changing either of these two options will change the monthly subscription price.

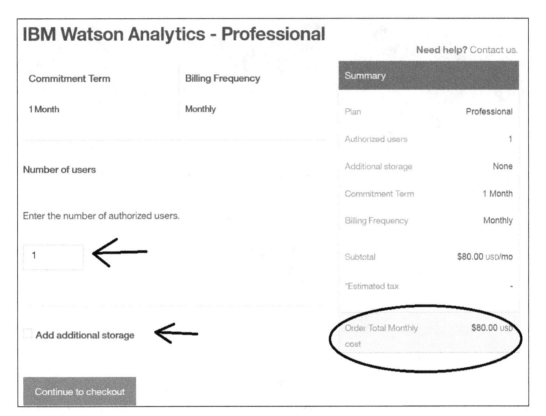

At the checkout (similar to any online shopping cart), you have to select a payment method, fill in the required information, and submit your order. That's all there is to it!

Watson Professional

Now that you've gone ahead and upgraded to professional, let's take a moment to examine some of the key differences between the *free* version and the *professional* version:

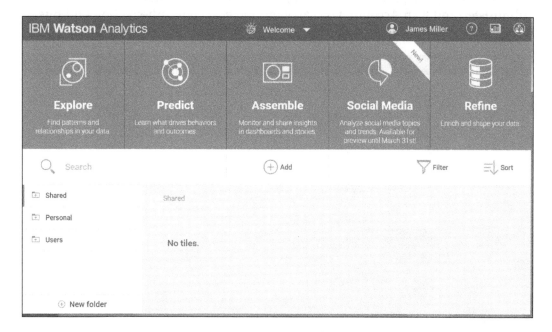

Available space

First, your maximum file upload size should have increased to 10 GB, and the maximum number of columns allowed in your dataset should now be 500. You can click on your name (in the top-right portion of the welcome page) and then click on **My Account** to verify this.

Administration – Account, Users, and Data connections

When upgrading to the Watson Professional version, you provided an *authorized user count* and (perhaps) additional storage. Now, when you click on your name, **Administer**, and then **Account**, you can view and edit your **Subscription Options** (check out the following screenshot):

From this page, you can see your current storage allocations and used space, the number of authorized licenses available and used, and a list of your purchases (from the cloud store). In addition, you can click on **Edit options** to visit the cloud store again and make more purchases.

Upgrade – related products

From the cloud store, you can also access two related products, Cognos Business Intelligence (BI) and SPSS modeler:

Docs

Once you have upgraded the documentation (docs) available, now include information and helpful hints on the features relevant to the Watson Professional edition, for example, **Adding BI Report data**:

Conversations

The Watson **Conversations** feature gives you the ability to act as a team by sharing commentary about data and visualizations—all *directly inside* of Watson. In addition, you have the ability to create polls—to collect users' responses to a specific question—and save all the responses with in the conversation.

Starting a conversation

To start a conversation, you must first have an existing (previously saved) asset open. Then click on the conversations icon (shown here):

After you click on this icon, the conversation panel (shown in the next screenshot) is displayed, where you can enter a new comment:

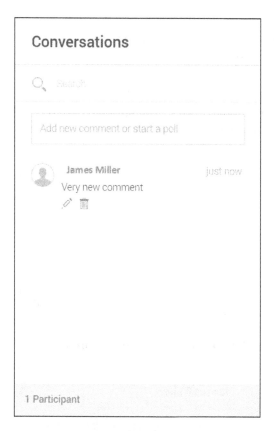

In the conversation panel, Watson displays all previously posted comments (along with the author's name, date, and a timestamp). Watson also gives a participant count at the bottom of the panel.

Once your conversation becomes lengthier, you may find it convenient to search and filter the comments. For example, you can locate all comments posted by a particular user by typing the @ symbol and then the first letter of their username.

For example, @J would return all comments that I posted using the username **James Miller**.

Keep in mind that the conversation you create for a particular asset is available only for that specific asset, and if you delete that asset, the entire conversation associated with it will also be deleted.

Polls

You can also create a *poll* to ask users a question about your data or visualization. To create a poll, click on the **Edit** icon (shown in the following screenshot) for a comment within your conversation:

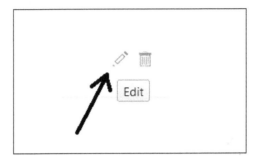

After you've clicked on the **Edit** icon, the **Create Poll** icon will be visible:

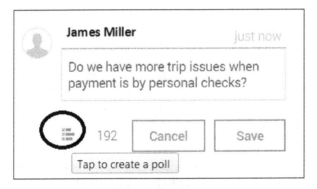

Once you click on the **Create Poll** icon, you can enter a *poll question* and any number of optional responses:

Finally, clicking on the **Save** button will create the poll:

Folders

Once you upgrade to the Professional edition of Watson, you can begin utilizing *folders* to organize your assets. Unlike the free version, Professional offers three types of folders: **Shared**, **Personal**, and **Users**. You may not have access to each of the different Watson user folders. Only administrators can see individual user folders. By default, each authenticated user will have a user folder in their own name. In the middle of the main Watson page along the left-hand side, you'll see the folder structure shown in the following screenshot. Clicking on a folder will display any subfolders that you have access to as well as the content (or assets) saved in that folder:

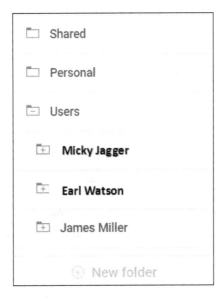

Watson also allows you to create new folders to better organize your assets by clicking on **New Folder**, after which you can enter a name for the folder, as shown here:

You can then *move* or *save* assets in your new folder, depending on the permissions set on the assets. Permissions of Watson assets can be set to the following:

- **View Only**: This allows users to open and view assets but not change them
- **Edit**: This allows users to view, edit, save, and delete assets
- **Full Control**: In addition to the permissions set for View and Edit, users can also set permissions on assets

Folders offer a nice way to organize your Watson assets. In addition, they can be used to share your assets with other users within your Watson account. Sharing can be accomplished simply by selecting the asset to be shared and then selecting **Move**. From there, the **Move asset** dialog box allows you to select the folder to move the asset to, like this:

 More details on the specifics of asset permissions can be found in the online docs.

Adding data source connections

The most exciting reason (in my opinion) for upgrading from the free version of Watson to Watson Professional is the *additional data sources*. In prior chapters, all of our sample use cases were based on CSV files. With Professional, we have many more choices to explore.

From the **Welcome** page (the *free* version), if you click on **Add** and then on **Upload Data**, you will see this:

In the *Professional* version, you see the following screen (note that **Browse** for locating and uploading a CSV file is still supported, but it is not shown in my screenshot here):

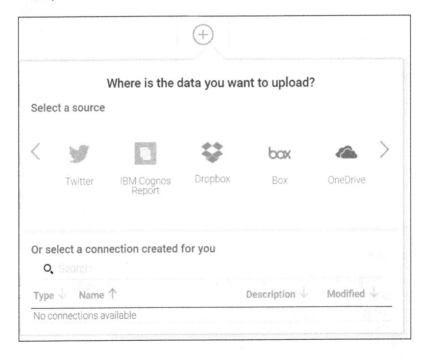

Select a source

Under **Select a source**, you have the following options for loading of data: **Browse** (also available in the free version), **Twitter** (also available in the free version), **IBM Cognos Report**, **DropBox**, **Box**, and **OneDrive** (all new options).

Or select a connection created for you

In Watson professional, you have the option to create datasets based on data that is contained in on-premises and in-cloud databases. With Watson administrator access, you can set up and manage external data connections so that you can access this type of data with Watson. From the *Where is the data you want to upload?* page, using the section named **Or select a connection created for you**, you can search for and sort the list of available connections by their type, name, description, and last modified date, as shown here:

Creating connections

Since we've just upgraded (to Professional), this page displays **No connections available**. To create a data connection, you need to be a *Watson administrator* for your account. From the Watson main page, click on the account icon, which is shown here:

Then click on **Administer**. You'll see that the administrator accounts are indicated in the user list with the crown icons to the left of the username, as shown in the following screenshot:

	Name ▲	Status ⇕	Last modified ⇕
	James Miller	Active	Jan 20, 2016
	Steven Spurr	Active	Jan 25, 2016
	Payton Mann	Active	Nov 2, 2015
	Thomas Bradys	Invited but not activated	Nov 2, 2015
	Earl Watson	Active	Nov 2, 2015

> Note that if you are not a Watson administrator, you will not be able to see the user list.

This is the *non-administrator* view:

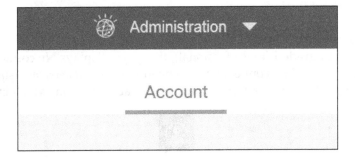

The following is the *administrator* view:

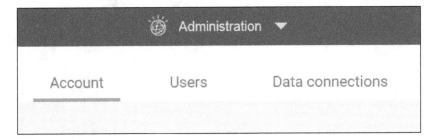

To create a data connection, an administrator can click on **Data connections** (shown in the next screenshot) and then on **Create new connection**:

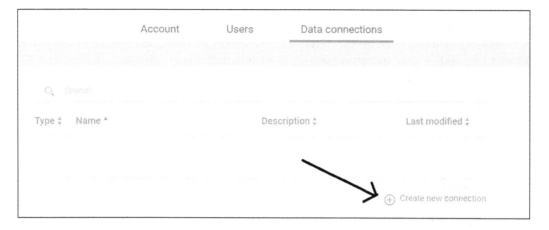

In the **Select a connector type** dialog, you can click on the data connection that you are interested in setting up, as follows:

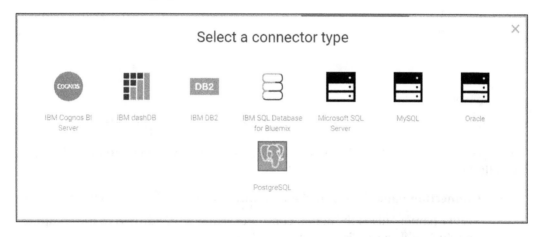

A sample connection – Microsoft SQL server

Let's take a look at setting up a data connection using Microsoft SQL server as an example. To create such a connection, you need to provide specific configuration information. From the **Select a connector type** dialog (shown in the preceding screenshot), you can click on the **Microsoft SQL Server** icon. Then, you can use the Watson Analytics *administration console*, as shown in the following screenshot, to set the required properties:

To keep things simple, the only required settings that you will need to provide are the following:

- **Connection name**: This is just an identifier for the connection within Watson
- **Server name**: This is the actual computer name or IP address of the computer on which SQL server is running
- **Port number**: This is the port number on which SQL server is running
- **Database name**: This is the name of the SQL server database that you wish to access

 Once you've provided the settings, it is a good idea to click on **Test** to make sure that the connection between Watson and the database works correctly.

Once your connection is set up, it will appear as an option for uploading data under the **Add** tab on the Watson main page, as follows:

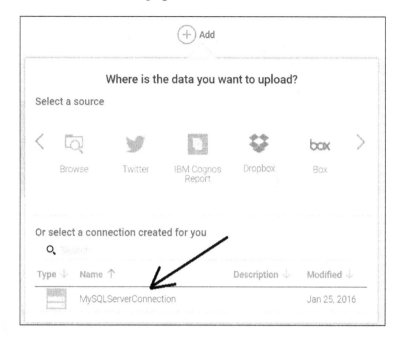

When you click on the data connection, Watson will prompt you for your user ID and password, like this:

Upon successful connection (to your database), Watson provides the **Import from data connection** dialog (shown in the next screenshot), where you can:

1. Type a SQL statement
2. Run the SQL statement and preview the results
3. Upload the SQL results to Watson:

Once your data is uploaded to Watson, you can explore, predict, or assemble it (and do much more) just like any other data file you have already uploaded!

Twitter

As we've already mentioned, the **Browse** and **Twitter** options are available in the *free* version of Watson. We have covered the use of **Browse** in several earlier chapters of this book, so let's now take a moment to talk about using Twitter data with Watson.

Once you click on **Add** (from the main page) and then on the Twitter icon, Watson displays the **Select the Twitter data you want** page (shown in the next screenshot), where you can create a custom query that Watson uses to search for data within Twitter:

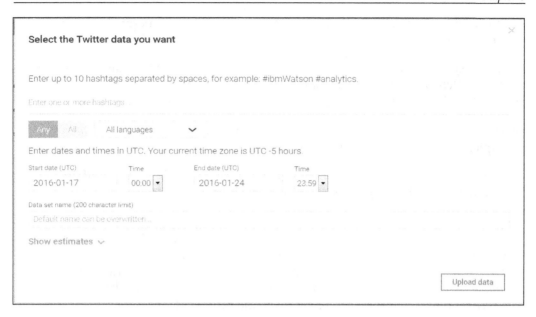

A couple of assumptions are required here; one is that you have a valid Twitter account, and the other is that you understand the concept of hash tagging. Let's look at a simple example.

I've created the following Twitter postulation, with which I'd like to use Watson to, perhaps, gain some insights. With the NFL season coming to an end, I've set the following parameters:

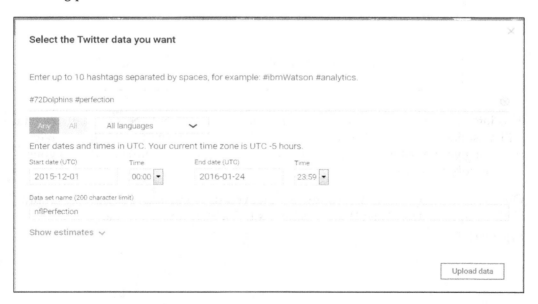

In the hashtag textbox, Watson allows you to enter up to 10 separate hashtags (each separated by a space). I've entered two: **#72Dolphins** and **#perfection**.

On the next line, you *qualify how Watson will use your hashtags*; for example, should Watson match tweets that contain *any of the hashtags* that you entered or only tweets that *contain all the hashtags* that you entered? In my example, I said **Any**.

In addition, you can filter your Twitter search by the *language the tweet is in*, for example, only English or only Chinese. In my example, I used **All languages**.

Next, you need to set a *span of time* for Watson to search within — a **Start date** and **Time** and an **End date** and **Time**. I went for **2015-12-01** to **2016-01-24**.

As you type your hashtags, Watson *adds* those tags to the **Data set name** textbox to be used as a name for the dataset (you are limited to 200 characters). I recommend changing the name to something that would be easily identifiable later when accessing the data, and hopefully the name you choose will be one that follows a *naming convention* that you have adopted (covered in *Chapter 7, Taking It to the Enterprise*). In my example, I am using the name **nflPerfection**.

Lastly, Watson provides a convenient feature that you can use to project the usefulness of the Twitter data based on the custom query that you just created.

Clicking on **Show estimates** (shown in the preceding screenshot) will provide you with the estimated number of tweets available (those that match your query's parameters that you set) as well as the *size* of the data file that will be created. Check out this screenshot for your understanding:

Hide estimates ∧

Number of tweets available: **7,130**   Size (MB): **2**

This information is invaluable. For example, if the number of tweets is small, the data will most likely not be useful, and the *size of the file* to be created will help you with managing your available space (based on how much size you purchased with your Watson subscription).

Once you are happy with the parameters that you have entered, you have to simply click on **Upload data**. Then Watson connects to Twitter, runs your query, and uploads your data:

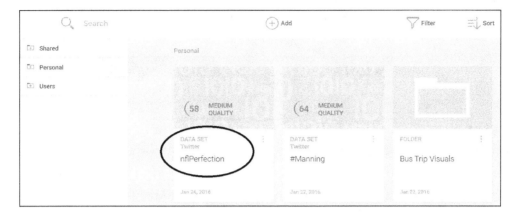

IBM Cognos BI

In Watson, you can directly access data that is retrieved as an IBM Cognos *list report*. To allow users to access that data, Cognos must be configured by a Cognos administrator.

Integration can mean many things. In fact, if the data that you want to analyze in Watson resides in Cognos BI, the simplest way to analyze it is to integrate it:

1. Log in to Cognos BI (this requires a Cognos user ID), as shown in this screenshot:

2. Run a report or query and format it as a **Delimited text (CSV)** file, as shown here:

3. Save the output, as follows:

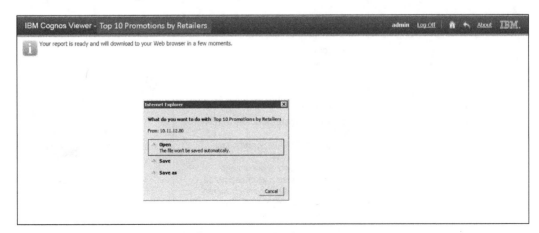

4. Upload your file to Watson (as a new dataset):

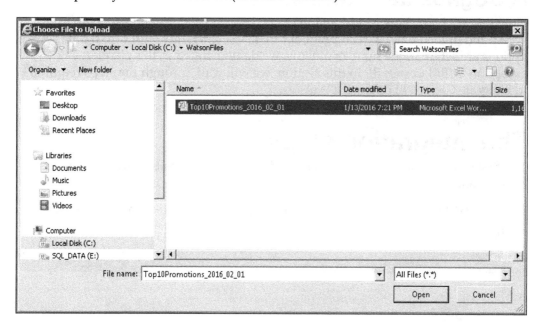

Voila! Simple integration!:

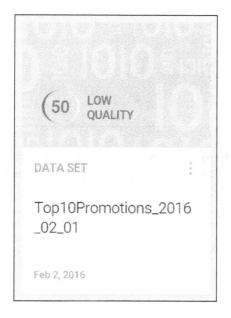

A Cognos data connection

Now that we know how to add and manage data connections and use them to access and upload data, we can point out that *most* (currently supported) data source options are set up in the same manner as we demonstrated in this chapter. One exception is *IBM Cognos BI*. In this section, we will walk through the steps required to integrate Cognos BI data with Watson.

The integration steps

The first step for integrating data that resides in IBM Cognos BI is to set up a data connection.

From the **Welcome** page, click on **Administer**, and then click on **Data connections**, as shown here:

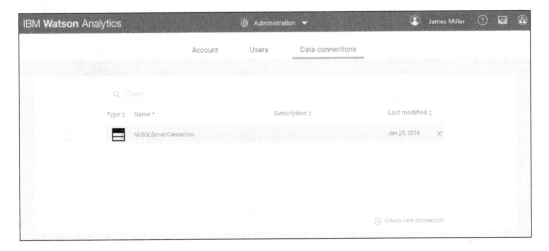

From here, click on **Create new connection**. Next (just as you would do for other types of data connections), select a connector type (this time **IBM Cognos BI Server**):

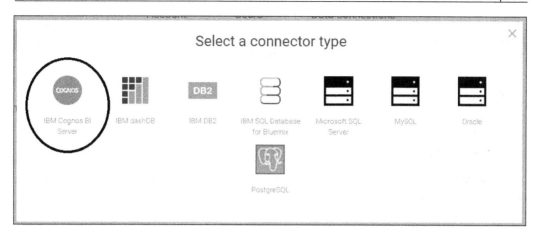

On the **Create new connection** dialog, enter a connection name and the URL for your Cognos BI or Cognos Analytics server, as shown here:

The *connection name* is just an identifier (make it something that, perhaps, describes the data you'll be accessing, rather than just the default). The URL must begin with `https://`, and this is the address of the Cognos BI server you will be accessing.

Again, as we did earlier when setting up our sample SQL server connection, you should click on **Test Connection** to verify that the connection information is correct and that the server is able to accept the connection.

Note that you may need to enter login information (as if you were logging in to Cognos BI directly). You might also need to connect directly to your Cognos BI or Cognos Analytics server in another tab or window of your browser (if the security certificate of your Cognos BI or Cognos Analytics server is not signed by a trusted certification authority).

Upon successfully connecting to Cognos BI, you will have a new data connection available in Watson, like this:

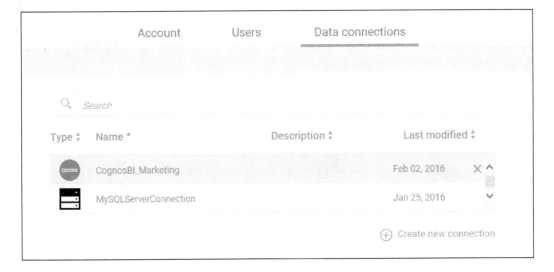

Although it may be considered by some to be more convenient to set up direct data connections to various data sources, such as SQL Server and IBM Cognos BI), I find that (at least if I am *not sure* what data I want to use) exporting data from these sources to a text (CSV) file, and then uploading that file, grants me more flexibility in that it provides me with the opportunity for data review and refinement before uploading to Watson. However, if a report or query is established within the source system that selects exactly the data in the exact format that you want, then a direct connection is the way to go.

More learning opportunities

To learn more *about* Watson, you have to *do more with* Watson, and that means continuing to explore with more and more different data samples.

Using you own data

You can download the sample data that was prepared for, and used in, the examples in this book. You can also search in the Watson Analytics community for other sample datasets of interest and, in addition, you can upload your own data.

No matter where your data comes from, keep in mind that before uploading, you should take a look at the data to see whether there are things you want to *improve* before uploading the data, in order to improve its overall quality and directly help Watson understand it. For example, you may want to:

- Remove blank rows
- Remove summary rows and columns
- Eliminate nested column headings and nested row headings

Available references and material

Always start with the basics. You should spend time checking out the Watson help menu. There, you will find that you have access to the following sources of information:

- Detailed topics under **Docs** (from the **Welcome** page, click on the **Help** icon and then on **Docs**)

- *Little Hints* that appear in various places in Watson (from the **Welcome** page, click on the **Help** icon and then click on **Show all hints**)

- Expert blogs, discussion forums, and sample data (from the **Welcome** page, click on the **Help** icon and then on **Community**)

- There is also a nice variety of informative videos available on YouTube at `https://www.youtube.com/user/watsonanalytics/videos`

Summary

In this chapter, we walked through upgrading to Watson Professional and adding direct data connections. We outlined the steps required to integrate Watson with IBM Cognos BI. Finally, we offered some ideas to continue increasing your understanding and expertise in IBM Watson.

We've now reached the end of our *introduction to IBM Watson* journey—a trip that started with answering the question *what is IBM Watson Analytics?* and has ended with you perhaps being able to incorporate Watson into your daily routine and confidently add it to your resume.

Good Luck!

Index

A

administration console 19
Application Programming
    Interfaces (APIs) 139 82

C

collections 20-22
Content Analytics
  about 85, 86
  automation 86
  frequency and deviation 87
  manual 86
  precision and recall 87, 88
  textual analysis, issues 86, 87
Content Analytics architecture
  about 17
  data flow 20
  deep inspection 21
  flow, exiting 20
  main components 18
Content Analytics data model
  about 57, 58
  collection process 64-69
  collections adding to, from assemble 69-81
  collections, building 64
  collections, multiple 63, 64
  data, categorized 59, 60
  data sources, multiple 60, 61
  date-sensitive data 61
  information, extracting from
      textual data 62, 63
  iteration, planning for 81
  relational mindset 58, 59
  sources, structured 59

sources, unstructured 59
conversations, Watson Professional
  about 198
  polls, creating 200, 201
  starting 198-200
correlation 22
crawlers 18
crawl space 18
Cycle of analysis, with Watson Analytics
  about 88
  actions, determining 90
  analysis, performing 89
  data, obtaining 89
  purpose, defining 88, 89
  validation 90

D

data appearance, customizing
  about 140
  column names, customizing 143
  column types, changing 140, 141
  custom reaggregation 142
  media, modifying 146
  persistence 144
  presentation styles, modifying 144, 145
  properties, modifying 145, 146
  themes, modifying 144, 145
  views 144
data considerations
  about 57
  Content Analytics data model 57, 58
data context
  about 28
  importance 29

for documentation 172
hints 173
object naming 173
natural language processing (NLP) APIs 82
natural text 21
node 156

O

objects
grouping 148-150
regrouping 148-150

P

particular application
customizing, reasons 139
extending, reasons 139
permissions, Watson assets
Edit 203
Full Control 203
View Only 203
points of interest
about 128-130
Assemble 130-136
versioning 130
prediction 107, 108
preparation 174
preprocess 174

Q

questions
building 27, 28
data values 27
for data 27
keywords 27
names of columns 27

R

references and material 219
requirements
fulfilling 139

S

search engine 19
searching 21

shortcut panel bar, IBM Watson analytics
about 7-11
Assemble 12-15
Explore 12-15
Filter 16
original starting point 15
Predict 12-15
Refine 12-15
Sort 17
visualization configuration 16
visual representation 15
structured text
versus unstructured text 21
subscription 140

T

tabs
using 147-150
templates
using 112-118
testing
about 173
before, sharing 174
text analytics 21
text data
about 104
data metrics 104
filter 106
search 105
Twitter 210-212

U

unstructured text
versus structured text 21
use case
defining 25
facilitation of validation 26
importance 26
promotion of quality 26
simple use case 118-128
understandable narratives 26
user concentration 26
Watson Analytics 26
use case examples
about 29, 157-166
context 51, 52

www.ingramcontent.com/pod-product-compliance
Lightning Source LLC
Chambersburg PA
CBHW082117070326
40690CB00049B/3599